WEIGHT LIFTING IS A WASTE OF TIME

WEIGHT LIFTING IS A WASTE OF TIME

SO IS CARDIO, AND THERE'S A BETTER WAY TO HAVE THE BODY YOU WANT

DR. JOHN JAQUISH
HENRY ALKIRE

LIONCREST
PUBLISHING

WEIGHT LIFTING IS A WASTE OF TIME
So Is Cardio, and There's a Better Way to Have the Body You Want

ISBN 978-1-5445-2100-8 *Hardcover*
978-1-5445-0893-1 *Paperback*
978-1-5445-0892-4 *Ebook*
978-1-5445-0894-8 *Audiobook*

DEDICATED TO PAUL JAQUISH

For years we watched and have begun to understand your unconventional and, most often, more elegant problem-solving methods. For those who ask us how you put a car on the moon (the lunar roving vehicle): The solution most often involves you going in the opposite direction of other inventors/engineers for the answers. You have taught us so much, and you are an inspiration to hold ourselves to a higher standard every day.

CONTENTS

FOREWORD

I've always loved working out, but at forty-three years old, after seven orthopedic surgeries and some hard conversations with orthopedic surgeons about joint replacement, lifting conventional weights just wasn't an option for me any longer. Fortunately, I met Dr. Jaquish, whose discoveries have allowed me to maintain size and strength without any damage to my joints. Now that I have begun to reinforce some of my damaged tendons and ligaments, strength is increasing for the first time in a long time.

Critics question Dr. Jaquish and his team for their unconventional approach to building strength, but anything truly revolutionary is always initially met with resistance. Personally, I've seen many fighters and athletes injure themselves with poorly conceived programs and improper technique. Dr. Jaquish's program is straightforward and relies on natural human movements. When you look at the approach of stronger variable resistance with no static weight at all, it makes sense with human biomechanics. Dr. Jaquish's research from the UK National Health Service (NHS) showed that people could exert sevenfold greater peak muscular output compared to the kind of weights they would lift in the gym. This is one of many studies cited in this book that has led me to believe that this system and the training techniques in it would be extremely helpful for athletes of any type. Other than competitive weightlifters and powerlifters, athletes shouldn't care about how much weight they lift. Lifting weights is a means to the ends of strength, power, and muscle mass. For instance, fighting is not a contest of who can lift the most weight but of who can show up on fight day with the greatest power-to-weight ratio and the lowest chance of injury.

If your goal is to gain strength and muscle with a program that is sustainable and is not irritating to your joints, then this is the book for you. The information in this book will get you closer to what you want than almost any conventional approach, even if you, like most people, don't have pain-free movement. Now if you DO have pain-free movement, then that only means you haven't injured yourself YET! Why not try a simpler, safer method all while improving joint health without the risk of injury? There are also some interesting, well-supported, cutting-edge, scientific advancements in this book that can help you improve almost every aspect of your life. The goal of this book is simply put: optimization, be it through diet, time-restricted eating windows, or strength training. At the end of the day, this book strives to help you become the best version of yourself.

Forrest Griffin
MMA Hall of Famer and former light heavyweight champion
Two-time *New York Times* bestselling author

INTRODUCTION

Do any of these describe your experience with exercise?

Problem #1: Lifting weights year after year without seeing visible results.

Problem #2: Sustaining injuries or experiencing chronic joint pain as a result of lifting weights.

Problem #3: Performing hours of cardio without significant weight loss or muscle gain.

Problem #4: Quitting exercise entirely or never starting a routine because you don't have enough time.

If you're like most people, at least one of these statements applies. Why? You might be surprised to learn your busy schedule isn't actually the problem, and neither is how long or hard you work at the gym—it's a gap in knowledge. Most exercise routines mistakenly rely on principles scientifically disproven as many as forty years ago. This creates a tremendous disconnect between how people exercise and what science shows us is the most efficient, effective way to work out and achieve measurable results.

What if you learned a better, faster way to build muscles and lose fat?

What if this method was scientifically proven, so you knew it was effective?

And what if—instead of the hours it takes to drive to the gym, work out, and then drive back again—your new regimen took approximately ten minutes a day and could be done at home with only a few key pieces of equipment?

Your problems with exercise would be solved. With the knowledge gap eliminated, you'd know exactly how to get the body you want, in far less time than you ever imagined.

If all that sounds good, keep reading. We've done the research and have the science-backed answers you need to start getting far better results with a workout even the busiest people can fit into their day.

ENGINEERING A DISRUPTION

As biomedical engineers, we didn't set out to disrupt the fitness industry. We weren't looking to debunk fitness recommendations that continue to exist despite a lack of scientific evidence regarding their efficacy. In the beginning, John was simply trying to help his mother manage a medical problem.

John's mom had been recently diagnosed with osteoporosis. Studies show a fifty-year-old woman presenting with similar bone loss to hers has a 2.8 percent risk of death related to hip fracture during her remaining lifetime—the same odds as dying from breast cancer.[1] Even when death is not the outcome, the statistics are grim. There is a 40 percent chance of never walking independently again, and up to a 20 percent chance of needing nursing home care due to that same potential broken hip.

John's mother was understandably upset at the news. However, while she wanted to get healthier, she also didn't want to take osteoporosis drugs. Common side effects of those include headaches, stomach pain, nausea, heartburn, fever and chills, pain while urinating, and dizziness. Less common side effects include rare cancers and osteonecrosis, a rare condition in which jawbone cells start to die off.

Most people faced with this situation would have a difficult choice to make: take the pharmaceuticals and hope to avoid the laundry list of unpleasant side effects, or forgo the drugs and hope to never fracture a bone. Luckily, John's mother isn't most people—she has a son with an avid interest in human physiology, and he happened to have a great teacher for problem-solving: his father. With those family members on her side, the prognosis was anything but typical.

John's dad was on the team that designed and built the Lunar Rover. He received more than 300 patents during his career. He even likes to wear his inventor hat at home, once creating a motion-detector sprinkler system to protect the family garden from scavenging animals that featured water pressure so high it could knock over an adult deer. Needless to say, animals went elsewhere after one experience with this system.

---

1 Cummings SR, Black DM, & Rubin SM. (1989) Lifetime risks of hip, Colles', or vertebral fracture and coronary heart disease among white postmenopausal women. *Arch Intern Med*, 149:2445.

So it's not surprising that upon learning of his mother's diagnosis, John did exactly what his father would do. Presented with a challenge, he became determined to find a solution. It was as complicated and simple as that.

SEEKING THE HIGHEST IMPACT

To solve this problem, John's first objective was to understand what environmental factors had a positive effect on bone density. He decided the best way to uncover this information would be to find people who were already outliers in this area. If there was some group of people achieving superhuman levels of bone density, he might be able to identify the behaviors that led to those results. And if he succeeded, maybe there would be a way to translate what he learned to help his mother.

He soon discovered his target population: gymnasts. People who participated in gymnastics had higher bone density than non-gymnasts of the same age, even if they quit the sport long ago.[2] John discerned that infrequent high impact force exposure was the key to their bone strength because it triggered an adaptive response of self-reinforcement in the bones, which is protective against progressively greater impact that could actually cause injury or fracture. This is the effect associated with practicing gymnastics.

Gymnasts encounter forces that most people may not even know the human body can withstand. For example, when gymnasts dismount from the uneven bars and land on the ground, the sudden deceleration creates impact forces that can exceed

2 Jürimäe, J., Gruodyte-Raciene, R., & Baxter-Jones, A. D. (2018). Effects of Gymnastics Activities on Bone Accrual during Growth: A Systematic Review. *Journal of Sports Science & Medicine*, 17(2), 245.

ten multiples of their body weight.[3] That means a 120-pound gymnast's musculoskeletal system might experience 1,200 pounds of loading, if only for an instant, when they engage in a fairly standard gymnastic movement.

Upon discovering this information, John began reading all of the loading and bone adaptation studies he could find. One of the earliest examples of this sort of research dates all the way back to 1892 in a paper describing the Laws of Mechanotransduction.[4] This work states that bones develop by adapting to stress much in the way muscle does. Another study included farmworkers who received higher levels of impact, where researchers observed adaptations through cadaver bone extraction. These studies seemed to confirm John's hypothesis, reinforcing his determination to move forward on this project.

Of course, John's mom wasn't going to take up competitive gymnastics in her seventies. Once someone's bones are structurally compromised by osteoporosis or osteopenia, it is hardly a safe option to begin jumping off of tall objects. However, John thought that creating a medical device that simulated these high impacts while eliminating associated risks was within the realm of possibility.

John began his quest to develop such a device by identifying the positions in which humans naturally absorb high impact forces. Next, he envisioned a device controlled by a robotic arm to reliably place individuals in these "impact ready" positions. Finally, he recognized the need for computer software to control

---

3 Marcus, R. (1996). Skeletal Impact of Exercise. *The Lancet*. November 1996. 384(9038): 1326-1327.

4 Wolff, J. (1892). *Das Gesetz der Transformation der Knochen*. Berlin, Germany; Verlag von August Hirschwald.

that process, provide biofeedback, and ensure the intervention could be consistently repeated over a series of many sessions.

With this vision in mind, John came up with a "cocktail napkin" drawing of his invention. On the surface, it may have looked similar to exercise machines seen in gyms, but in reality, it was quite distinct in functionality from any existing equipment. The proposed medical device was grounded in emulating the amount of impact humans absorb when doing gymnastics.

In envisioning a sophisticated osteogenic loading apparatus designed to measure and deliver the amount of force necessary to trigger bone growth, John had begun to crack the code to decreasing and possibly even reversing osteoporosis.

INVENTING A WORLD-CHANGING MEDICAL DEVICE

However, he still needed assistance in designing and building a prototype. Although he was working on his PhD in Biomedical Engineering at the time, the project required *electrical* engineering knowledge—something he did not possess. His father's mechanical engineering abilities and National Instruments, a multinational producer of instrumentation and test equipment, proved helpful in this phase of development. Over the next several years, John iterated through several different design concepts for an osteogenic loading device.

Several years later, a hospital in London purchased one of John's osteogenic loading devices and carried out a research study testing that device on post-menopausal females diagnosed with osteopenia or osteoporosis. The results were even more promising than John had hoped. Deconditioned women in their fifties and sixties were creating force of up to nine times their body weight on the device. This is well beyond the force a professional weightlifter can produce using traditional weightlifting equipment, and out-of-shape women were doing it relatively easily with minimal risk of injury.

Around this time John brought Henry Alkire, an eighteen-year-old aeronautical engineering student at Cal Poly, on board as an intern. Along with other scientific research he was involved in, Henry spent the next several years working with John on product design for subsequent iterations of osteogenic loading devices. After a long period of careful development, the current commercial version of OsteoStrong's Spectrum System—the Robotic Musculoskeletal Development System (RMDS)—was born.

The Spectrum System allows OsteoStrong centers to deliver precise body positioning where higher impact forces can be naturally absorbed in four key areas of the body: upper, lower, core, and postural. Users engage in four brief but maximum force presses and lifts that are somewhat similar to the deadlift, abdominal crunch, chest press, and leg press. In this way, the Spectrum System produces axial bone compression throughout the entire skeleton.

Most bones require a force of at least two times body weight to trigger an adaptive response. Research published in 2012—years after John's hypothesis was developed—suggests 4.2 multiples of body weight is the minimum force required to build bone density in the hip joint.[5] While conventional weight training can only generate peak forces just approaching 1.5 times body

---

5 Deere, K., Sayers, A., Rittweger, J., & Tobias, J. H. (2012). Habitual levels of high, but not moderate or low, impact activity are positively related to hip BMD and geometry: results from a population-based study of adolescents. *Journal of Bone and Mineral Research*, 27(9), 1887-1895.

weight, OsteoStrong is designed to deliver impacts of many multiple times a user's body weight, essentially turning on the switch for bone growth.[6]

Based on his internship experience, Henry changed his major from aeronautical to biomedical engineering and continued working with John throughout college. He graduated Cal Poly on a Friday, was back to work with John on Monday, and is now listed as coinventor on the patent for OsteoStrong.

As for John's mother? She no longer has osteoporosis, and the osteogenic loading devices have since been placed in over 300 clinics worldwide, helping over 600,000 individuals with their bone health. One study on these devices demonstrated over 14 percent bone density gains in both the spine and hip as a result of one year of once-weekly treatments taking less than ten minutes each.[7]

You can see the dramatic changes graphically here (baseline to post hip and spine force output differences in twenty-four weeks).

---

6 Ferguson, B. (2014). ACSM's guidelines for exercise testing and prescription 9th Ed. 2014. *The Journal of the Canadian Chiropractic Association*, *58*(3), 328.

7 Hunte, B., Jaquish, J., & Huck, C. (2015). Axial Bone Osteogenic Loading-Type Resistance Therapy Showing BMD and Functional Bone Performance Musculoskeletal Adaptation Over 24 Weeks with Postmenopausal Female Subjects. *Journal of Osteoporosis & Physical Activity*, 3(146), 2.

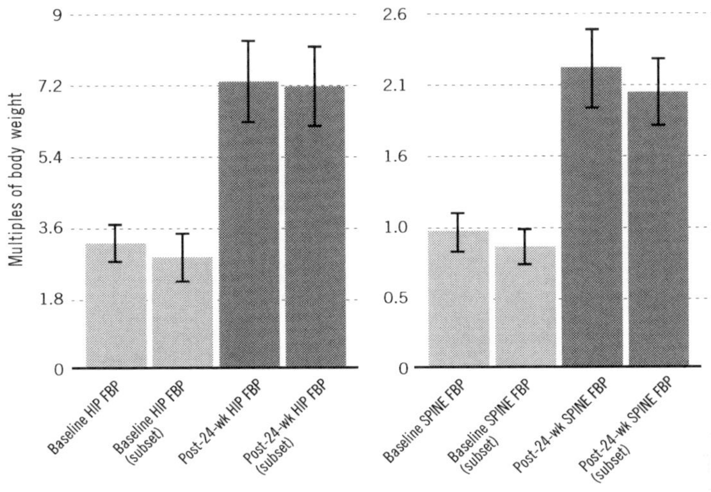

FROM BONES TO MUSCLE

In our pursuit to solve John's mother's medical issue, we ended up inventing the most effective bone density building medical device available. OsteoStrong's efficacy was recently confirmed through research, most recently involving scientists at NASA's Johnson Space Center at the University of Texas Medical School,[8] and OsteoStrong is now partnered with Tony Robbins for rapid clinical deployment of the technology. But the story doesn't end there.

As a direct result of testing done with OsteoStrong, John became the first scientist to fully quantify the maximum capacities for muscular output. Cross-referencing OsteoStrong user data with exercise statistics compiled annually by the American College of Sports Medicine, he determined a sevenfold difference between the average muscle load created in a typical fitness environ-

8 Tsung, A., Jupiter, D., Jaquish, J., & Sibonga, J. (2021). Weekly Bone Loading Exercise Effects on a Healthy Subjects Strength, Bone Density, and Bone Biomarkers. *Aerospace Medicine and Human Performance*, 92(3), 201-206.

ment—on weight machines and when weightlifting—and what we are actually capable of doing.[9] He then took this information a step further, plotting a detailed force curve identifying peak capabilities throughout the entire range of motion, from weak to strong.

Consider a bench press. The weakest range is when the arms are fully contracted at the beginning of the lift, when the bar is just above your chest. The medium range occurs midway through the lift, with the barbell in between its highest and lowest position for the repetition. The strongest range is at the top of the rep, where the arms are nearly fully extended but the joints are not locked. Each range is capable of handling a different amount of weight. The strong range is where it gets easiest and feels lightest—and consistent with that sensation of lightness, this is where the muscle has the most capacity to produce force.

A light bulb went on: Weightlifting has everything backwards. It doesn't give people the results they're looking for because it can't provide the amount of force necessary to trigger muscle growth throughout the entire range of motion. Our weight choice is limited to what our weak range can handle, so we're not effectively working our medium and strong ranges. Worse, when we choose a weight that better fits those stronger ranges, we sustain injuries because the weak range is where the most cumulative joint damage occurs. Weightlifting overloads joints, which increases the chances of injury and forces us to subconsciously hesitate, and NEVER achieves anything close to full engagement of the target muscle. Weights don't change the force they put on you as you move by any magnitude, let alone a calculated one. See the force output capacity in different positions.

---

9 Ferguson, B. (2014). ACSM's guidelines for exercise testing and prescription 9th Ed. (2014). *The Journal of the Canadian Chiropractic Association*, *58*(3), 328.

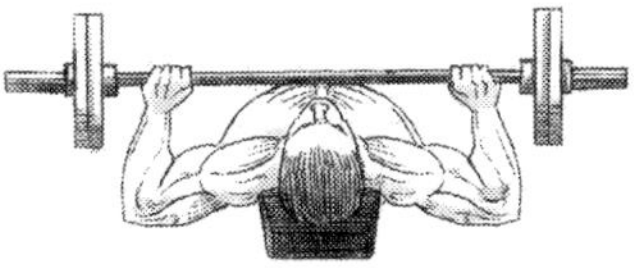

WEIGHT/FORCE = X

This is the place in a movement with the lowest force capacity.

WEIGHT/FORCE = 2X

This is the place in a movement with greater force capacity, yet very limited compared to the impact-ready range.

WEIGHT/FORCE = 7X

This is the place of maximum force capacity for output, hence this is how we brace for a fall.

WEIGHT/FORCE = NULL

While force can be tolerated here, the bones support the majority of the weight thus the muscles are offloaded.

This is why we say weightlifting is a waste of time.

We know this is a controversial statement and one that may make people shocked or angry. However, John's peak force power curve clearly demonstrates that people have a vast amount of unused muscle capability that weightlifting can't begin to stimulate.

LEADING A FITNESS REVOLUTION

So what is needed to maximize muscular growth and optimize the inefficiencies of weightlifting? A weight that changes as we move, giving us a lighter load in the weaker/joint-compromised ranges of motion, normal heaviness in the middle ranges of motion, and a tremendously high weight in the impact-ready ranges of motion. This was the way to achieve the level of engagement we now knew the muscle is capable of based on John's research.

This realization led to the creation of the second invention: X3.

X3 is an exercise system that builds muscle much faster than conventional lifting, in far less training time, and with the lowest risk of joint injury. It delivers varying weight throughout the range of motion, triggering your muscles to adapt and change much in the way OsteoStrong triggers bone growth. X3 marks the beginning of a physiologically, scientifically sound shift in the fitness industry. Some could argue this is the first time science has ever been applied to fitness from a specific movement standpoint.

In this book, we will show you a tremendous amount of data supporting just how poor a stimulus weight training is for its intended purpose, as well as a tremendous amount of data showing how variance in resistance is the obvious answer to this challenge. We'll also show you how variance in the proper proportion will grow muscle and change body composition faster than you might ever imagine possible—we've even seen users experiencing visible muscular gains by the week.

We are also going to disseminate the actual science behind important fitness questions, eliminate common misconceptions, and show you how to use this newfound knowledge to create the body you want. By the time you're finished reading, you will have learned:

- What variable resistance is and why it's superior to weightlifting
- What triggers muscle adaptation

- How to accelerate muscle growth and fat loss
- How to trigger the right hormonal responses through exercise
- How to eat properly for muscle gain and fat loss
- Why so many people exercise but do not see results
- What's different about the X3 fitness system, why it works, who uses it, and their results

By no means are we claiming to have discovered the solution—this is applied science. You'll still have to work hard to get results. And you'll still have to be mindful of your dietary choices and eat properly to achieve optimal outcomes.

But the upside is your workout will take only ten minutes a day using proper form and equipment (not to save you time, but because this is actually optimal for growth), can be done at home, and delivers far superior results.

CHAPTER 1

WHERE WEIGHTS WENT WRONG

While inventing the osteogenic loading devices, John developed a deep understanding of the impact-ready ranges of motion. ("Impact-ready" refers to the ranges your reflexes would choose in order to absorb high forces experienced in hard contact with the ground.) Approaching the subject with the ultimate goal of stimulating bone growth required taking a different perspective than prior researchers. By determining where peak forces occur in relation to body placement on the OsteoStrong device, John was able to plot the strength curve throughout the range of motion in a way no scientist had before.

A CLOSER LOOK AT RANGE OF MOTION

We've already briefly introduced the concept of the different ranges of motion using a standard bench press as an example. The same can be done for any movement, whether single-joint or multi-joint.

Take a push-up. The weakest range of motion is when your arms are bent and your nose is almost to the ground. Right before the arms come to full extension marks the strongest range of motion. Anyone who has ever attempted a push-up knows there is a vast difference in strength between these two positions.

For this reason, people often end up using only the top range of motion where the movement is easiest when doing push-ups. Everyone subconsciously does this to maximize reps, even children. If you watch a high school physical education class, you'll notice a percentage of kids won't go all the way down to where their nose touches the ground. They only do what they see as the easy part at the top, because that's where more muscle is usable.

Let's look at a deadlift. The weakest position is when you're bent over, the bar is near the ground, and your spinal erectors, hamstrings, and trapezius are elongated. The medium range is in the middle of the movement and the strongest is just before you're standing up. We're making the qualification of "just before" because if you lock out the joint, the muscles essentially turn off. Ever watched a professional mover move furniture and how they use moving straps? They change the length of the strap so they can engage with movements in JUST the optimized range.

The squat is another example. The weakest range is when your knees are the most bent and your body is closest to the ground. Just before full knee extension, as you approach the top of the lift, is the strongest range of motion. Sprinters subconsciously know this one. Does a sprinter use a full range of motion when contacting the ground to push off for the next stride? Absolutely not. A sprinter uses seven degrees of flexion behind the knee when contracting, yet has 180 degrees available. This is the range of efficiency where force delivery through the muscle is optimized.

WEIGHTS ARE FOR THE WEAK (RANGE)

John was the first to discover the sevenfold difference between the weakest and strongest range, effectively demonstrating that muscular capacity is far greater than anyone ever realized. His findings also exposed the Achilles' heel of weightlifting: Because the weight used is determined by the weakest range, there is a vast mismatch between the amount of weight lifted and our actual muscular potential. What's more, the stronger a lifter gets, the more cumulative damage to joints, since they are at their maximum possible capacities in the weakest range of motion. This causes pain and stops the muscle from contracting effectively through the process of neural inhibition (a concept we'll cover in greater depth in upcoming chapters).

Lifting a weight light enough to accommodate the weak range means the mid and strong ranges aren't being worked to anywhere near their full capacity. Choosing a weight heavier than what your weak range can handle isn't effective either, because it ensures you can't complete a single rep. It also increases your risk of injury. As a result, weightlifting ends up fatiguing the least amount of tissue possible based on the limitations of the weakest range of motion.

Some people think low-force, high-repetition exercise—doing three sets of fifty curls with two-pound weights, for example—is the solution to this problem. However, research shows muscle is not built through low forces. In fact, you can actually greatly diminish muscle exercising this way. In a 2016 study, researchers concluded that when it comes to training for muscle strength and hypertrophy, "a trend was noted for the superiority of heavy loading."[10] What does this mean? It means that when you want

10 Schoenfeld, B. J., Wilson, J. M., Lowery, R. P., & Krieger, J. W. (2016). Muscular adaptations in low-versus high-load resistance training: A meta-analysis. *European Journal of Sport Science, 16*(1), 1–10.

to grow muscle in the most effective way possible, there is no getting around HEAVY.

Other people try to focus their training on the weaker range in an attempt to activate more muscle there. This, they reason, will eventually balance out the mismatch of power among the ranges of motion. Unfortunately, that is not how the body works, and here is why:

1. As we've stated before, the weak range is where joints are at the greatest amount of risk and most prone to injury. For example, the bottom of a deadlift is where people tend to injure their backs, sometimes resulting in permanent damage.
2. Research demonstrates muscle does not effectively fire in the weak range. A recent electromyography study on pectoral activation during bench press showed the nervous system is actually unable to recruit as much muscle tissue at the "sticking point," where the bar is closest to the chest.[11] As the movement progresses through the medium and strong ranges, increasingly more muscle is activated. Two studies have shown this neurological inhibition (often called neural inhibition) in the weak range is an evolutionary mechanism to protect joints when the muscle is in a compromised position.[12,13]

This is common knowledge among neurologists, but many in

11 Van den Tillar R & Ettema G (2010). The 'sticking period' in a maximum bench press. *The Journal of Sports Science*, Mar 28 (5): 529–35.

12 Sterling, M., Jull, G., & Wright, A. (2001). The effect of musculoskeletal pain on motor activity and control. *The Journal of Pain*, 2(3), 135-145.

13 Pageaux, B. (2016). Perception of effort in exercise science: definition, measurement and perspectives. *European Journal of Sport Science*, *16*(8), 885-894.

the sports science industry have little familiarity with the concept. Unfortunately, that means athletes who follow the "power through the pain" theory only end up making their problems worse by adding to their chronic/long-term joint damage.

The increased possibility of injury coupled with the fact that the human nervous system makes complete muscle recruitment a physiological impossibility at the weakest range proves the training is not a sound investment of your exercise time. If muscle is not firing/activating, there can be no benefit. You're just fighting against nature.

HIGHER WEIGHT, HIGHER RISK

Serious/elite weightlifters understand gains don't come from working on the weakest muscle range. They therefore try to lift as heavy as possible during their exercise routines. Unfortunately, "high force" in the context of static weightlifting still means "high for the weak range of motion." Chronic soreness of the joints along with more serious injuries occur as a result.

The most typical overloading injury we see is tendinitis of the elbow, also known as golfer's elbow or tennis elbow. Shoulder and knee problems are common as well. These injuries are indicative of damaged cartilage and are cumulative and permanent.

We've worked with experienced weightlifters who have been training hard for decades. They've certainly spent enough time and energy to see significant results when it comes to physique and strength. The problem is they also suffer a myriad of biomechanical issues—they're almost all injured in some way. People who have been doing heavy squats for many years can barely get out of a chair without tears coming to their eyes. They were seeking health and ended up with long-term, debilitating knee pain instead.

THE SOLUTION: VARIABLE RESISTANCE

Sustaining injuries and underutilizing muscle tissue are symptoms of weightlifting's biggest weaknesses: it overloads joints and underloads muscles. In no other type of functional movement would a human voluntarily attempt to deliver the same force through an entire range of motion. If someone had a piano to move, they wouldn't bend their back as much as possible and pick it up from the lowest point available because that would maximize the opportunity for injury *and reduce their lifting capacity*. But that's exactly how people exercise, and the logic just doesn't add up. Clearly, a more effective training protocol would be one that challenges muscle where we are most capable and takes stress off joints where we are least capable.

What's more, being limited to the weak range of motion's capacity seriously limits results. There's untapped potential a fixed weight cannot stimulate because the weight is constant while our muscle force output capability is variable. To create greater strength, the tissue in the medium and stronger ranges needs to be completely fatigued as well.

Matching our differing capacity with an appropriate level of resistance throughout the range of motion instead of using a constant weight chosen for our weakest point would make far more sense. For example, what if the weights got heavier as you got to the top of a bench press? What if the weights got lighter at the bottom of a deadlift? Delivering peak force at all ranges would certainly result in a better muscular response—in far less time—than conventional weightlifting.

This type of exercise, called variable resistance, already exists. In fact, it's been around for quite a while. So why wasn't everyone doing it?

CHAPTER 2

HOW VARIABLE RESISTANCE WAS UNDERESTIMATED

Even though John's original research centered on stimulating bone growth, his findings also set the stage for a new and aggressive way to look at human strength capability. His conclusions had incidentally quantified the absolute maximum outputs for humans engaging their major muscle groups. These maximum force production capacities were pinpointed in a multitude of different positions throughout the range of motion for several different standard exercises.

Bone loading is induced by and dependent on the supporting musculature, and he'd already proven muscles could withstand far greater forces than weightlifting can generate. Based on this discovery, we split our focus between bones and muscle. We started by taking a deep dive (as researchers, we call this a literature review) into the ways in which variable resistance had been applied in the world of exercise.

After culling through the available studies, we located numerous ones identifying variable resistance's superiority to weightlifting.

This held true whether the subjects were athletes or sedentary, old or young. All of which led us to wonder: why was everyone still lifting weights when variable resistance had been proven more effective at developing musculature?

TRIPLE THE GAINS

One of the most compelling variable-resistance studies was carried out at Cornell University. Participants were recruited from the men's basketball and wrestling teams, as well as the women's basketball and hockey teams. The student-athletes were tested both pre- and post-experiment for lean body mass, one repetition maximum back squat and bench press, and peak and average power.

Each was then randomly assigned to a control group or an experimental group. The control group continued an existing weight training protocol using standard barbells loaded with iron plates. The test group did an identical workout on the same equipment, only with bands added to the barbells. The average resistance was kept the same for all participants, so the experimental group lifted less actual "iron" to make up for the added resistance provided by the bands.

After seven weeks, the group using variable resistance recorded twice the amount of improvement on bench press single rep max than the control group and triple that on squats, as well as posting a three times greater average power increase. Even though the student-athletes were all performing the same exercises, participating in the same protocol, and lifting the same relative amount of weight, the variable-resistance group experienced significantly more strength gains than the weightlifting-only group.[14]

---

14 Andersen, CE, Sforza GA, & Sigg JA. (2008). The effects of combining elastic and free weight resistance on strength and power in athletes. *The Journal of Strength and Conditioning Research*, Mar; 22(2): 567-74.

VARIABLE-RESISTANCE STUDIES DONE WITH ELITE ATHLETES

NOTE: Pay close attention to the studies done with elite athletes, even if you are not one. Elite athletes have much more trouble building muscle than beginners to strength training. Therefore, when a study is done with them, it is a more important indication of what actually works. They are also more likely than other test groups to actually follow the protocol because they are more serious about their progress. In addition, most elite athletes participating in research are members of college sports organizations that do performance-enhancing drug (PED) testing. Conversely, many studies using average recreational exercising populations allow for self-reporting of exercises and nutrition, and the average population is not always honest about deviating from the prescribed exercise protocol or diet.

The effects of variable resistance on the maximum strength and power were tested using Division I football players. Here, volunteers from Robert Morris University were divided into three groups: One training with elastic bands, another with weighted chains, and the last using a traditional bench press. Each participant did a speed bench press and one repetition maximum test pre- and post-experiment. After seven weeks, the groups training with elastic bands and weighted chains—the athletes exercising with variable resistance—showed greater improvements than the ones working out on conventional weightlifting equipment.[15]

Another study of elite athletes sought to determine whether

15 Ghingarelli JJ, Nagle EF, Gross FL, Robertson RJ, Irrgang JJ, & Myslinski T. (2009).The effects of a 7-week heavy elastic band and weight chain program on upper-body strength and upper-body power in a sample of division 1-AA football players. *The Journal of Strength and Conditioning Research*, May; 23(3): 756-64.

higher loads of variable resistance resulted in bigger strength gains. Division II basketball players were recruited during the off-season to complete this research. Power development, peak power, strength, body composition, and vertical jump height were measured pre- and post-experiment. Participants were then divided equally into two groups. One added variable resistance to their training once weekly while the other continued doing traditional weightlifting only. At the end of the study, the athletes doing variable resistance posted significant improvements in speed, strength, vertical jump, and lean mass over the control group.[16]

Still more proof that variable resistance builds strength faster and more effectively than traditional weightlifting comes from a study of elite youth rugby players. The participants were tested for velocity and power on bench press before, beginning, and at the end of the study. A control group used free weights only while the other received 20 percent of their prescribed load on bench press from elastic bands. At the end of six weeks, the group using variable resistance showed bigger increases in their velocity, power, and one rep max on bench press than the free weight-only group.[17]

Yet another study, this time involving Division II baseball players, showed variable resistance provided greater rates of strength gain as measured by improvements at standard bench pressing. Even more importantly, participants doing variable resistance had less shoulder stress, enabling them to train fur-

---

16 Joy JM, DeSouza EO, Lowry R, & Wilson JM. (2013). Performance is increased when variable resistance is added to a standard strength program. *The Journal of Strength and Conditioning Research*, May; 30(8).

17 Rivière M, Louit L, Strokosh A, & Seitz LB. (2017). Variable Resistance Training Promotes Greater Strength and Power Adaptations Than Traditional Resistance Training. *The Journal of Strength Conditioning and Research*, April; 31 (4): 947–955.

ther, harder, and continue to gain muscle/strength at a faster rate than their peers due to the lack of neural inhibition and reduced risk of joint injury.[18]

In 2018, a group of professional rugby players participated in a randomized, controlled trial. This study measured explosive pushing power, something of critical importance in the sport. With only seven days of training time, the variable-resistance test group had statistically significant increases in pushing power, whereas the control group did not.[19]

Andersen, Fimland, and other researchers conducted two studies (2016/2019) evaluating different levels of variance with "high-level strength athletes, performing two different important multi-joint lifts, the squat and the deadlift." These assessed muscle engagement and rate of muscle recruitment by analyzing electrical activity through electromyography. As they began to raise the ratio of peak force in the strong, or impact-ready, range of motion, researchers noted increasing muscle engagement.[20,21] In other words, the greater the variance of resistance they used, the greater the peak muscle activation.

The most recent study with elite athletes is perhaps the most

---

18 McCurdy, K, Langford, G, Ernest, J, Jenkerson, D, and Doscher, M. (2009). Comparison of chain- and plate-loaded bench press training on strength, joint pain, and muscle soreness in Division II baseball players. *Journal of Strength and Conditioning Research*. 23: 187 195.

19 Godwin, M. S., Fernandes, J. F., & Twist, C. (2018). Effects of Variable Resistance Using Chains on Bench Throw Performance in Trained Rugby Players. *The Journal of Strength & Conditioning Research*, *32*(4), 950–954.

20 Andersen, V. Fimland, M. S., Kolnes, M. K., Jensen, S., Laume, M., & Saeterbakken, A. H. (2016). Electromyographic comparison of squats using constant or variable resistance. *The Journal of Strength & Conditioning Research*, *30*(12), 3456–3463.

21 Andersen V, Fimland MS, Mo D-A, Iversen VM, Larsen TM, Solheim F, et al. (2019) Electromyographic comparison of the barbell deadlift using constant versus variable resistance in healthy, trained men. PLoS ONE 14(1): e0211021.

shocking in terms of how far behind the rest of the world is in terms of using variable resistance to build muscle. In a survey of Norwegian powerlifters, 76.9 percent reported using variable resistance as a part of their regular training program.[22] Those who follow international powerlifting will know that Norway may be one of the strongest nations in the world per capita.[23]

At this point, John knew some researchers were working on closing the gap between random levels of variance and the absolute maximums seen in his 2015 research.

VARIABLE-RESISTANCE STUDIES DONE WITH SEMI-ATHLETIC INDIVIDUALS

The studies using elite athlete populations add strength to the library of variable-resistance literature in general. Almost identical results have been seen using more "average gym-goer"-type individuals.

One such study had two groups exercise, one using variance and the other standard weights. Cronin and researchers discovered greater EMG activity during the later stages (70-100 percent) of the eccentric phase (meaning the lowering of resistance) of the banded squat when compared to a standard weight squat. Their ten-week analysis showed banded resistance training led to significant improvements in lunge performance (21.5 percent)

---

22 Shaw, M. P., Andersen, V., Sæterbakken, A. H., Paulsen, G., Samnøy, L. E., & Solstad, T. (2020). Contemporary Training Practices of Norwegian Powerlifters. *Journal of Strength and Conditioning Research*, 10.1519/JSC.0000000000003584. Advance online publication, https://doi.org/10.1519/JSC.0000000000003584.

23 Contreras, B. (2017, January 2). An interview with Marte Elverum - A Women's Norwegian Elite Powerlifter. Retrieved from https://bretcontreras.com/an-interview-with-marte-elverum-a-womens-norwegian-elite-powerlifter/.

compared with control groups. In this study, the variance group outperformed the control by 21.5 percent in ten weeks.[24]

A 2019 study by Smith et al. looked at sensory reflex performance after a multi-week exercise program that compared a variable-resistance group to one using standard weights. The variance group exhibited greater reflex improvements, and the study concluded: "variable resistance training elicited greater reflex adaptations compared to dynamic constant external resistance."[25] This indicates that speed improvements could result with variable resistance, perhaps because more muscle tissue is activated. Further, if more muscle tissue is able to balance an individual as they move, this is a direct driver of one's ability to sprint with greater proficiency. Consistent with this hypothesis, another 2019 study showed variable resistance was able to activate more muscle and positively influence jump performance after just one intervention, but the standard weight training control group did not demonstrate any influence for the same kind of test.[26]

As mentioned earlier, to gain strength and muscle size there is no getting around HEAVY. Although what is considered heavy is different for every individual, most studies have seen sixty seconds as an optimal time under tension before fatigue. Obviously with variable resistance, you benefit from more force than you can achieve with ordinary fixed weightlifting for any

---

24 Cronin, J, McNair, PJ, and Marshall, RN. The effects of bungy weight training on muscle function and functional performance. *The Journal of Sports Science*, 21: 59-71, 2003.

25 Smith, C. M., Housh, T. J., Hill, E. C., Keller, J. L., Anders, J. P. V., Johnson, G. O., & Schmidt, R. J. (2019). Variable resistance training versus traditional weight training on the reflex pathway following four weeks of leg press training. *Somatosensory & Motor Research*, *36*(3), 223-229.

26 Mina, M. A., Blazevich, A. J., Tsatalas, T., Giakas, G., Seitz, L. B., & Kay, A. D. (2019). Variable, but not free-weight, resistance back squat exercise potentiates jump performance following a comprehensive task-specific warm-up. *Scandinavian Journal of Medicine & Science in Sports*, 29(3), 380-392.

given exercise time. But don't just take our word for it. Instead, consider this quote from yet another relevant study on variable resistance: "Squatting with elastic bands facilitates more weight used and time under muscle tension."[27]

VARIABLE RESISTANCE AND UNTRAINED INDIVIDUALS

We've often encountered the objection that the research just cited only proves variable resistance works for athletes. To answer that, we'll begin by pointing out the obvious: The benefits of exercise enjoyed by athletes are available to non-athletes as well. In fact, deconditioned individuals may respond even more quickly to a new exercise protocol because there is greater room for improvement.

We can also point to existing variable-resistance research on non-athletes demonstrating similar efficacy to studies done on athletes. For example, forty-five middle-aged, sedentary women were tested on knee push-ups, sixty-second squats, and body composition. They were then divided into two groups, one using elastic bands to exercise and the other weight machines. All performed the same exercises and number of repetitions, as well as used the same perceived effort, twice a week for ten weeks.

At the end of the study, both groups recorded less body fat, more lean mass, and increased reps for push-ups and squats.[28] Because very low-resistance bands were used, results were fairly

27 Rogers, N. L., Gene, J., Juesas, A., Gargallo, P., Gene, A., Salvador, R., … & Rogers, M. E. (2018). Squatting with elastic bands facilitates more weight used and time under muscle tension. *Medicine & Science in Sports & Exercise,* vol. 50:no. 5S:pp 50.

28 Colado JC & Triplett NT. (2008). Effects of a short-term resistance program using elastic bands versus weight machine for sedentary middle-aged women. *Journal of Strength and Conditioning Research,* September; 22(5): 1441-8.

similar between the variable-resistance and weight-training groups. But even at very low levels that reached nowhere near muscular capability, variable-resistance training proved quite effective.

Another recent study of thirty-eight post-menopausal women showed training with bands not only significantly lowered weight and waist circumference, but also improved cardiovascular profiles and cholesterol indicators. The control group that didn't do any exercise over the same one-year period showed significant *increases* in their weight and waist circumference.[29] It's safe to say that most of us want to be leaner and healthier, not fatter and more prone to heart problems. Variable resistance is a proven method of achieving these goals.

Other research shows variable resistance offers a low joint stress method for facilitating greater muscular engagement. A study involving people with an injured anterior cruciate ligament found that "anterior cruciate ligament strain values obtained during squatting were unaffected by the application of elastic resistance intended to increase muscle activity."[30] This is consistent with our hypothesis that variable resistance permits exercisers to load their muscles with greater forces while reducing stress on joints.

If you don't belong to any of the demographics we've discussed so far, take heart. We haven't encountered any test population

---

29 Gomez-Tomas C, Chulvi-Medrano I, Carrasco JJ, & Alakhdar Y. (2018). Effect of 1-year elastic band resistance exercise program on cardiovascular risk profile in post-menopausal women. *Menopause*, September; 25 (9): 1002-1010.

30 Beynnon, B. D., Johnson, R. J., Fleming, B. C., Stankewich, C. J., Renström, P. A., & Nichols, C. E. (1997). The strain behavior of the anterior cruciate ligament during squatting and active flexion-extension: a comparison of an open and a closed kinetic chain exercise. *The American Journal of Sports Medicine*, 25(6), 823-829.

that doesn't seem to benefit from variable-resistance training. Even older adults (60+) have been tested and show similar results to both the elite populations and more average exercisers.[31] Variable resistance works no matter your current conditioning, age, or sex. The principles it follows and muscle tissue it stimulates remain the same.

ISOLATING VARIABLE RESISTANCE AS THE KEY FACTOR

Many of the studies we just discussed compare standard weightlifting protocols to those including some level of variance, provided by either rubber/latex banding or other methods. For example, a given control group may have exercised with weights only and their corresponding test group may have used a lighter weight with elastic banding connected to the weight bar to offer a small level of variable resistance to the entire exercise movement. In every test of this kind cited, the variance group outperformed the static resistance one. So, what is the critical variable that changed—the variance or something about static resistance? The obvious answer is variance.

Other studies had test groups using bands only, with no fixed weights at all. In those cases, we also observed the test group using variable resistance outperforming the control group using fixed weights. In these cases, the situation is even simpler. We don't have to ask what factor is more important, we just have to look at what methodology yielded superior results—and that is consistently variable resistance.

---

31 Komiyama, T., Muramatsu, Y., Hashimoto, T., & Kobayashi, H. (2016). Estimating the Effect of Dynamic Variable Resistance in Strength Training. In *International Conference on Intelligent Robotics and Applications* (pp. 26-35). Springer, Cham.

In all cases, the group that included variance performed better, became stronger, and grew muscle mass faster. So what's more important? Weights or variance?

A gym in Ohio that trains competitive lifters applied variable resistance to its lifting protocols and ended up breaking over 140 world records. When asked how they were doing it, the answers were a bit convoluted. Perhaps they were protecting their method for business reasons, to keep an advantage. But aside from this outlier, why didn't the world immediately jump on variable resistance after most of these studies were published?

RESEARCH AND INNOVATION ARE NOT THE SAME THING

John actually had one of the researchers referenced in this chapter approach him at the National Congress of the American College of Sports Medicine (ACSM) to share his excitement over the technology/products John had been working on. Then he asked, "How did you figure it out?" John was confused because the real question in his mind was, "How did the rest of you guys NOT figure this out?" Of course, he never said this, and ended up buying a round of drinks for the other researchers instead.

There is a tremendous difference between research and innovation. The job of a researcher is to test a concept that might be slightly (or greatly) different from the standard approach to a given objective. In the context of exercise science, they are often testing a concept that someone else invented, which has already been used to some extent in practice. Then they test the two concepts and control for outside variables that might skew the data one way or the other. The conclusion to the test involves calculating if there was a statistically significant difference between the two data sets and commenting on other observations that may have been made during the study, which can enhance everyone's understanding around that particular subject matter.

Notice that nowhere in this process is the researcher mandated to create anything or consider how their research findings might be used in the process of product development. In the variable-resistance field, for example, a 2016 study concluded that variable resistance (or as the authors described it, "accommodating resistance") would be useful for improving the training efficacy of powerlifters, bodybuilders, and athletes.[32] The conclusion never segued into product design planning, because that's just not what researchers typically set out to do.

An obvious exception to the above assessment of researchers would be R&D engineers employed by large companies for the express purpose of performing research with the goal of product development. But even when you include this group, successful research-driven product innovation is surprisingly rare. How long before the advent of high-quality consumer digital cameras was the first prototype developed in an R&D setting? The answer is about thirty years. In fact, Eastman Kodak invented the functioning digital camera in 1975 (yes, that Kodak) but they initially decided not to develop it into a product. Because there aren't that many people out there looking to challenge convention and take the risks inherent to innovation, they waited decades before turning that research into an actual product.

As you likely know, eventually other businesses developed this

32 Kompf, J., & Arandjelović, O. (2016). Understanding and overcoming the sticking point in resistance exercise. *Sports Medicine, 46*(6), 751-762.

technology on their own, and competition from digital cameras made by other manufacturers drove Kodak to file for bankruptcy in 2012. This is just one example of the gap between research and actual product development. It strongly suggests there are other areas of academic understanding right now that do not coincide with, and are more advanced than, the products or methods people generally use.

These are innovations waiting to happen.

WHY THE UNTAPPED POTENTIAL?

An absolutely critical limitation to developing the ultimate variable-resistance system was that the studies were lacking data describing the optimal amount of variance to use. Meaning, some studies used X amount of weight in the weak range, then 1.2 X amount of weight in the impact-ready/stronger range. Other studies used slightly different ratios, and even still, some other studies didn't even bother to fully quantify the degree of variance they were using. The lack of hard numbers and ratios for the maximum amount of desired variability in a variable-resistance protocol likely deterred innovators from developing a real variable-resistance product. We use the word "real" because we do acknowledge there are a number of junk/fake fitness products that use elastic banding, but these can deliver only five to thirty pounds of force, which is not relevant for any type of strength application.

For John, developing the ultimate variable-resistance system was straightforward, given the circumstances. He had already invented the world's most powerful bone-density treatment device, so he wasn't afraid of taking the risks in creating a new concept. Most importantly though, the bone density data allowed him to start with the answer to a question no one had yet asked. When the data was collected in the 2015 London hospital study, he knew he was the only one who could see just how far variable resistance could be taken.

No one else in the fitness world had this data and an understanding of strength adaptation. Only John did. With this knowledge, he forged ahead.

CHAPTER 3

OPTIMIZING OUR HORMONES AND GROWTH FACTORS

We'd just uncovered one large knowledge gap in fitness—the superiority of variable-resistance strength training over traditional weightlifting—when we discovered yet another. We were amazed to find in the context of exercise and body composition, the role of hormones was not widely discussed or understood by people engaging in exercise, or even by many of the people acting as experts in the field. There seemed to be a big disparity between what people in the scientific community had learned about this subject and how that knowledge has been incorporated—or more accurately, not incorporated—into exercise programs. Whatever the reason, we were excited to explore the connection between hormones, fat, and musculature.

And when we say "hormones," we don't mean Performance Enhancing Drugs (PEDs). We stipulate this because, throughout our journey, we've encountered many people who believe everything related to fitness is a scam. They think people who are in great shape were either born that way or took steroids to obtain their physiques. These are ludicrous assumptions, particularly that last one. Thousands of years ago, sculptors were carving statues of lean, muscular people. Clearly the ancient Greeks weren't using anabolic pharmaceuticals to achieve visible musculature.

In truth, body composition is most effectively changed when the right hormones are released to facilitate muscle building and lipolysis. The hormones designed to retain fat become suppressed. Perhaps ironically, users of PEDs are quite adept at leveraging these facts to great effect through illegal exogenous hormones, albeit with potentially serious, even lethal consequences. By contrast, regular exercisers tend to craft their exercise routines with little regard for hormonal impact. This is a great loss because, given the proper stimulus, hormone production can happen readily and naturally in the body, and natural exercise-induced hormonal changes do NOT carry the same dangers as illegal PED use. What's more, the specific fitness routines that create the proper hormonal environment for weight loss and muscle gain are not excessively complicated and may come as a surprise—especially to people who rely on cardio for weight control.

THE CARDIO-CORTISOL CONNECTION

It's a common misconception that cardio is an effective way to lose body fat. In reality, it can have the opposite effect of what people typically want or expect—prolonged cardio can keep you fatter, for longer. That's because cardio stimulates cortisol, the body's natural stress hormone.

Cortisol can promote two effects to undermine your fitness goals. First, it has the potential to inhibit lipolysis, thereby protecting body fat. Second, it can promote proteolysis, including the breakdown of lean muscle tissue.

Why might cardio-type exercise promote those effects? Doing hours of cardio tells the body that it needs to go long distances with a limited amount of fuel. It responds by protecting that fuel, holding onto fat as long as possible.

Think of your central nervous system as an engineering team working to ensure you are optimized for your environment. Optimization for cardio requires carrying excess body fat to power your efforts. It means minimizing muscle because muscle has significant caloric requirements.

It is very stressful to run for hours on end, and that effort takes quite a toll on the body. This is why marathon runners, although thin, have very little muscle and a surprising percentage of body fat. They're the epitome of what is referred to as "skinny fat," or as we like to call it, "cardio fat."

WHY CARDIO FOR WEIGHT LOSS IS A LIE

There is a plethora of existing research that indicates cardio is not a particularly effective way to lose weight, despite what most of us were taught to believe. Certainly there are other health benefits to cardiovascular exercise, but weight loss isn't one of them.

A 2001 literature review examined the effect of exercise on weight loss and total body-fat percentage. The studies included were then categorized as either short term (less than sixteen weeks in duration) or long term (lasting more than twenty-six weeks). In each, participants did a minimum of 1,100 calories worth of exercise per week. Regardless of the length of the experiment, the review showed exercise produces rather underwhelming results—weight loss of small fractions of a pound per week (0.04 pound to 0.18 pound in the long-term groups) with minimal impact on body fat.[33]

A similar meta-analysis pointed to the same conclusion. This one looked at sixteen existing studies investigating how weight is affected by exercise. Within this body of research, results showed the average *total* weight loss attributable to exercise alone is between one and two kilograms. We think most people would agree three or four pounds—especially over longer periods of time—is not a compelling return on your exercise investment, and for those who are substantially above their healthy weight, not a sufficient result either.[34] Worse yet, both reviews included several randomized, controlled trials that showed no statistically significant effect at all for the exercise intervention in the context of weight loss. This is strong evidence that typical exercise routines vary between ineffectiveness and marginal efficacy, and it underscores our argument that the status quo for exercise recommendations is not yielding compelling results.

These research results are consistent with our understanding of the hormonal effects of cardio. Like traditional weightlifting, it seems cardio gets everything backwards. It *increases* cortisol, which holds onto fat for fuel and *decreases* growth hormone production and promotes the reduction of muscle mass.[35] This is definitely not what people want or expect from their fitness routine.

---

33 Janssen I & Ross R. (2001). Physical activity total and regional obesity: Dose-response considerations. *Medicine & Science in Sports & Exercise*, June; 33(6 Suppl): S521 – 7.

34 Wing RR. (1999.) Physical activity in the treatment of the adulthood overweight and obesity: current evidence and research issues. *Medicine & Science in Sports & Exercise*, November; 31(11 Suppl): S547-52.

35 Nishida, Y., Matsubara, T., Tobina, T., Shindo, M., Tokuyama, K., Tanaka, K., & Tanaka, H. (2010). Effect of low-intensity aerobic exercise on insulin-like growth factor-I and insulin-like growth factor-binding proteins in healthy men. *International Journal of Endocrinology.*

We know many individuals will be disappointed by these findings because they have always thought cardiovascular exercise was fantastic for so many reasons. It still *is* fantastic if your goal is to be able to run or bike or swim long distances. But you need to realize you may be weaker and hold on to more body fat as a result, which for most people is not acceptable.

Let's review from a logical perspective why cardiovascular exercise is a driver of muscle loss and body fat maintenance. Again, think of the central nervous system as an engineering team that is always trying to optimize you for the environment you are in by triggering the endocrine system (hormones) to make adjustments based on environmental sensory perception. This means that if you regularly put yourself in a position where you are running great distances, your nervous system is going to make adjustments to your hormone levels to help you get better at that activity/environment. The question then becomes: what changes should be made to optimize your physiology for running great distances?

Here's how an engineering team designing a car to go great distances would make design decisions, and how the body seeks to achieve the same objective:

- **Lighten the chassis.** Low weight means traveling greater distances. From a human physiology perspective, this means sacrificing bone density. This hypothesis may not be something commonly associated with exercise. However, it is consistent with research on the subject, which indicates that endurance athletes typically DO have low bone density.[36]
- **Shrink the engine.** A smaller engine burns less fuel going

36 Hind, K., Truscott, J. G., & Evans, J. A. (2006). Low lumbar spine bone mineral density in both male and female endurance runners. *Bone, 39*(4), 880–885.

the same distance. There is a reason economy cars don't have V12 engines. What would be the human physiology parallel to this? What's the engine of the human body that drives its speed and ability to move? The answer is muscle. That's why with endurance athletes, cortisol becomes upregulated so muscle mass can be reduced, and the growth hormone is downregulated (growth hormone is protective of muscle loss, as you will read more about later in this chapter). It's much easier to go further on a given amount of caloric energy when you have less muscle tissue to contract as you move.[37,38] (*Note: If you read the previous two references, you'll observe one associated salivary cortisol with increasing muscular weakness whereas the other examined serum cortisol increases in response to endurance exercise. This difference in measurement types does not undermine our hypothesis, because research also shows specifically in the context of cortisol response to endurance exercise, "the strong intraclass correlation coefficient between 24 h cortisol versus SAL (salivary measurement) and SER (serum measurement) suggests that either sample can be used to monitor cortisol hormones during a recovery period from exercise training."*[39] *In other words, when it comes to endurance exercise-induced cortisol response, salivary and serum measurements are robustly correlated and either can be utilized for overall cortisol response measurement.*)

- **Add fuel storage.** If you want to go long distances, you need

37 Schwarz, L., & Kindermann, W. (1989). β-Endorphin, catecholamines, and cortisol during exhaustive endurance exercise. *International Journal of Sports Medicine, 10*(05), 324-328.

38 Peeters, G. M. E. E., Van Schoor, N. M., Van Rossum, E. F. C., Visser, M., & Lips, P. T. A. M. (2008). The relationship between cortisol, muscle mass and muscle strength in older persons and the role of genetic variations in the glucocorticoid receptor. *Clinical Endocrinology, 69*(4), 673-682.

39 Neary, J. P., Malbon, L., & McKenzie, D. C. (2002). Relationship between serum, saliva and urinary cortisol and its implication during recovery from training. *Journal of Science and Medicine in Sport, 5*(2), 108-114.

a big fuel tank, right? Well, the fuel tank of the human body is body fat. This is another reason why cortisol is upregulated. Higher cortisol levels are associated with more and longer-lasting body fat storage.[40]

Your nervous system makes the adjustments needed to optimize you for the environments you put yourself in. That's why cardiovascular/endurance exercise can make you weaker, with less muscle mass and more body fat. While the evidence has existed for a very long time, as you can tell from the dates on all of the references above, this information still has not made it into the fitness industry's recommendations.

Why? Well, one possible explanation relates to the fact that they sell a lot of treadmills and exercise bikes. As Upton Sinclair famously said, "It is difficult to get a man to understand something when his salary depends upon his not understanding it!"

TESTOSTERONE

While the growth hormone can protect existing muscle, even during periods of caloric deficit, testosterone is critical for muscle growth. Building muscle is one of the best things you can do to enhance your health because lean tissue has a synergistic relationship with every organ in the body. The more musculature you have, the more efficient the delivery of nutrients to the organs.

Along with muscle growth, testosterone is one of the largest drivers of cardiac health. There is more testosterone absorption in cardiac muscle (the heart) than there is in any skeletal

40 Moyer, A. E., Rodin, J., Grilo, C. M., Cummings, N., Larson, L. M., & Rebuffé-Scrive, M. (1994). Stress-induced cortisol response and fat distribution in women. Obesity Research, 2(3), 255-262.

muscle in the body, based on the more than doubled capillary density of cardiac tissues.[41] Some endocrinologists have surmised the heart may have far more testosterone receptors than first thought, which can explain how low testosterone is a strong indication of a shorter life. One highly cited study concluded, "Testosterone insufficiency in older men is associated with increased risk of death over the following 20 yr., independent of multiple risk factors and several preexisting health conditions."[42] Without enough testosterone, people are not only at risk for cardiac issues but chronic depression, obesity, and a loss of both hair and libido.[43]

Testosterone is anabolic, so it promotes growth. It works well with the anti-catabolic protective properties of growth hormone. Although men trigger more testosterone upregulation than women, the effect remains the same insofar as the hormone still contributes to muscle growth in both men and women. However, because the amount of active testosterone receptors someone has and the available testosterone to populate them influences the degree to which muscle strength and size can be built, men experience a much greater average muscle-building response.

This results in the obvious differences in muscle mass typically seen between men and women. It also means that women who are weightlifting should not expect to be building a physique comparable in muscle mass to male weightlifters. Based on the questions we receive from customers and potential custom-

---

41 Marsh, J. D., Lehmann, M. H., Ritchie, R. H., Gwathmey, J. K., Green, G. E., & Schiebinger, R. J. (1998). Androgen receptors mediate hypertrophy in cardiac myocytes. *Circulation, 98*(3), 256-261.

42 Laughlin, G. A., Barrett-Connor, E., & Bergstrom, J. (2008). Low serum testosterone and mortality in older men. *The Journal of Clinical Endocrinology & Metabolism, 93*(1), 68-75.

43 Giltay, E. J., van der Mast, R. C., Lauwen, E., Heijboer, A. C., de Waal, M. W., & Comijs, H. C. (2017). Plasma testosterone and the course of major depressive disorder in older men and women. *The American Journal of Geriatric Psychiatry, 25*(4), 425-437.

ers, this should come as a great relief to the majority of the population.

GREATER STRENGTH AND MUSCLE THROUGH TRIGGERING TESTOSTERONE

The major hormones responsible for weight loss and muscle gain—growth hormone and testosterone—are optimally stimulated through strength training. The levels released are primarily affected by the amount of force going through the body, or more specifically force going through a group of muscles in a kinetic chain (muscles working together for a movement in which humans normally engage). Using lightweight bands, doing Pilates, or similar high repetition, low-weight exercises often does not provide enough force to trigger a hormonal response or any growth response at all.

We've already mentioned it, but it bears repeating: if you want muscle to grow, there is no getting around HEAVY. You have to use a weight where you are unable to continue repetitions after thirty to sixty seconds. In terms of traditional weightlifting, we now know "going heavy" puts us at a higher injury risk because we are forced to choose a weight based on our weakest range; otherwise we couldn't complete one repetition. It's important to review the literature that shows the relationship between the more extreme weight a person can handle in an exercise and the upregulation of testosterone:

- Only maximal but not submaximal weightlifting significantly increases testosterone.[44]

44 Linnamo, V., Pakarinen, A., Komi, P. V., Kraemer, W. J., & Häkkinen, K. (2005). Acute hormonal responses to submaximal and maximal heavy resistance and explosive exercises in men and women. *Journal of Strength and Conditioning Research*, 19(3), 566.

- These results indicate high power resistance exercise can contribute to an anabolic hormonal response with heavier training, and may partially explain the muscle hypertrophy observed in athletes who routinely employ high-power resistance exercise.[45]
- Testosterone-to-cortisol ratio changes appear to improve with the presence of overload for the purposes of building muscle mass, meaning the highest levels of fatigue.[46]

One seemingly conflicting study compared three groups of exercisers training at different levels of weight: one group using four reps per set, another using six, and the third using ten reps. Since maximal weights influence testosterone the most, we should assume the low-rep sets produced the highest levels of testosterone. That's not how it went down, though. The results showed the ten-repetition protocol resulted in a far higher level of testosterone.[47]

The researchers pointed out that the exercise times for the other groups were very explosive and short. By comparison, the ten-repetition sets were slower and more controlled because greater balance is required to complete a higher repetition set. Beyond that, explosive, fast power-lifting-type movements have a large motor skill/neurological activation component. This means someone who does not train for speed in a movement does not build that skill. (We'll explain more about the neurology and association of speed training and testosterone with muscle

45 Fry, A. C., & Lohnes, C. A. (2010). Acute testosterone and cortisol responses to high power resistance exercise. *Human Physiology*, 36(4), 457-461.

46 Mangine, G., Van Dusseldorp, T., Feito, Y., Holmes, A., Serafini, P., Box, A., & Gonzalez, A. (2018). Testosterone and cortisol responses to five high-intensity functional training competition workouts in recreationally active adults. *Sports*, 6(3), 62.

47 Crewther, B., Cronin, J., Keogh, J., & Cook, C. (2008). The salivary testosterone and cortisol response to three loading schemes. *The Journal of Strength & Conditioning Research*, 22(1), 250-255.

mass in later chapters.) Therefore, the perceived stress for the ten-repetition protocol may actually have been the highest and produced the most muscular engagement over time, thereby reconciling with the previous studies.

These findings led to another realization about variable resistance: individuals are able to train with more force than they would ever be able to with regular weight training—and at the same time continue the set for longer because they're dealing with less weight in the weaker ranges of motion and thereby eliminating the sticking point/hardest point of the movement. This results in greater fatigue of muscle and greater testosterone effect. As we learned in the previous chapter, variable resistance provides a more effective method of delivering the appropriate amount of force throughout all ranges of motion.

Research supports an increased hormonal response through variable resistance compared to weightlifting. For example, in one study participants were measured both pre- and post-experiment for testosterone and growth hormone. Participants then performed the same exercise protocol using either bands or weights. Results showed the variable-resistance group using bands experienced a greater increase in both testosterone and growth hormone than those performing traditional weightlifting.[48] This is also consistent with research showing that variable-resistance-based loading of the strong range of motion leads to drastically increased peak muscle engagement.[49]

---

48 Walker S, Tiapale RS, Nyman K, Kraemer WJ, & Hakkinen K. (2011). Neuromuscular and hormonal responses to constant and variable resistance loadings. *Medicine & Science in Sports & Exercise*, January; 43(1): 26–33.

49 Nijem, R. M., Coburn, J. W., Brown, L. E., Lynn, S. K., & Ciccone, A. B. (2016). Electromyographic and force plate analysis of the deadlift performed with and without chains. *The Journal of Strength & Conditioning Research*, 30(5), 1177-1182.

GROWTH HORMONE

When you're young, growth hormone helps you do just that—grow. As adults, it assists in the regeneration of the body and cells. In addition to protecting muscle mass and promoting body fat loss, growth hormone is involved in tendon, ligament, and skin repair. For those reasons, we'd argue that it should actually be called "repair hormone" in adulthood.

Growth hormone is anti-catabolic towards muscle tissue, meaning it protects the tissue by preventing it from being broken down, such as for energy. This characteristic is different from being anabolic, which is when a hormone actually stimulates tissue growth. It is also in contrast to the potential proteolytic effect of cortisol, which can *encourage,* rather than prevent, the breakdown of muscle tissue.

In addition, growth hormone has lipolytic effects, meaning it promotes the breakdown of body fat for energy, even while its anti-catabolic properties simultaneously safeguard muscle. This is how exercise and nutritional habits that promote growth hormone production by the body can allow you to lose fat and maintain lean tissue mass at the same time—or even gain lean tissue while reducing body fat (more on this in Chapter 6).[50]

STABILITY IS THE SECRET SAUCE

Applying heavier loads under higher forces through variable resistance is one key to the natural upregulation of testosterone. Stabilization is another when it comes to growth hormone. By stabilization, we mean the body's natural reflexive muscle firing that occurs to keep you upright and stable.

---

50 Rasmussen, M. H. (2010). Obesity, growth hormone and weight loss. *Molecular and Cellular Endocrinology, 316*(2), 147–153.

This sort of muscle activation occurs automatically and without conscious involvement, and the magnitude of stabilization firing is consistent with common sense principles. If you stand perfectly still, relatively little, if any, stabilization is required. If you stand on an oscillating or unbalanced surface, more muscles have to fire more frequently to keep you upright and (relatively) stationary. What's more, if you are also carrying a heavy object, it places even greater demands on your muscles. Requiring the body to stabilize itself during an exercise stimulates a greater amount of muscle tissue, and the stabilization process itself activates special spinal reflex arcs meant for this purpose, which in turn appears to encourage increased hormone release.

Consistent with this, certain exercises are more effective in triggering a hormonal response than others. For example, squats are superior to leg presses. In one study, participants were separated into two groups and then did similar leg exercises in a three-set, ten-repetition maximum protocol. At the end of the experiment, the group that did squats showed a 634 percent increase in growth hormone while the ones doing leg presses showed no increase at all—even though they were lifting more weight than the squat group.[51]

This is because squats require your body to stabilize both itself and a heavy weight while it moves through space. With heavy lifts, some of this reflexive stabilization firing may cause you to feel like your muscles are shaking during the exercise. This is just an amplification of normal stability firing, and more weight means more stability firing. By contrast, in a seated leg

51 Shaner AA, Vingren JL, Hatfield DL, Budnar RG Jr, Duplanty AA, & Hill DW. (2014). The acute hormonal response to free weight and machine weight resistance exercise. *The Journal of Strength and Conditioning Research*, April; 28 (4): 1032–40.

press, there is no balance or stability component at all. This study provides robust evidence that growth hormone release is not triggered simply by exercise, or by high forces imposed upon muscle (as is the case with testosterone), because the leg press offers both of those attributes. What the leg press lacks is the requirement for reflexive muscle activation for stabilization purposes.

We took this knowledge a step further by conducting our own meta-analysis of twenty-three published data sets. What we found was stabilization activity increases growth hormone production anywhere from 200 percent to 2,600 percent. The specific amount is determined by a combination of loading plus stability: the greater the load, the greater the stabilization firing, the greater the hormonal response. What's more, this response is reflexive.[52] By conducting our own meta-analysis, we were able to define this principle of stability firing and its connection to growth hormone regulation.

THE SPRINT EFFECT: GROWTH HORMONE AND CORTISOL OPTIMIZATION

Have you ever noticed the head of a distance runner bobs up and down during a run while a sprinter's head remains stable at all times? These body mechanics help account for the differing hormonal responses between the two activities. A sprinter's head stays stable due to stability firing in just about every muscle of the body. The more stability perceived by the central nervous system, the more muscle becomes involved, and the faster the sprinter can go.

---

52 Jaquish J. & Alkire H. (2016). Stabilization Motor Reflex Activation and Acute Growth Hormone Response: A Systematic Review. *Journal of Steroids and Hormonal Science*, July; 7(3).

Sprinting, or doing high-intensity bursts of exercise with rest in between, does the exact opposite of prolonged cardio. Instead of keeping fat on the body by stimulating cortisol, this type of exercise optimizes hormone release by upregulating growth hormone. Clearly, if your desire is to be a champion distance runner, you don't want to carry a lot of muscle because it will slow you down. But if you want to lose fat and build muscle, high-intensity exercise is the way to go.

People often do both strength training and cardio in tandem, thinking these will combine to make them a stronger, better athlete. The problem is the two activities have conflicting goals and hormonal responses. While strength exercise upregulates growth hormone, cardio downregulates it. As a result, you end up working harder for suboptimal results, or in the worst cases, no gain at all. The exercises cancel each other out.

Even experienced sprinters work out for only twelve minutes a day.[53] They don't run for distance or do any other type of activity to intensify their training because that would stimulate the wrong hormones. Instead, they do frequent short bursts of exercise and get the muscular benefits that come from upregulating growth hormone.

Let's return to the analogy used earlier, comparing the central nervous system to an engineering team that is trying to optimize you based on the environment you place yourself in. So here, instead of trying to turn you into a machine that can go long distances, the nervous system is trying to develop you into a sprinter because you are practicing the activity of sprinting. So imagine this engineering team/nervous system is now trying to

53 Striet, P. (2020, February 1). Running 101: Getting Started With Sprints. Retrieved March 5, 2020, from https://www.livestrong.com/article/557767-running-101-getting-started-with-sprints/.

make you into a more sprint-type car/human (think Formula 1). Here are the design decisions it would make:

- **Strengthen the chassis.** A heavier frame is required to tolerate great power. From a human physiology perspective, this means increasing bone density, which is associated with sprint-type impacts, through the lower extremities. John's first book is about this subject.[54]
- **A more powerful engine.** A larger, more powerful engine can deliver faster performance in terms of speeds and acceleration. What would be the human physiology parallel to this? What's the engine of the human body that drives its speed and ability to move? The answer is muscle. This is why sprinters have more muscle on average compared with distance runners. They need the mass to produce the power to move faster. The nervous system perceives this environment and upregulates testosterone to facilitate added muscle mass. Sprinters can absorb/produce over four multiples of body weight,[55] compared with distance runners typically dealing with a little over two multiples of body weight.[56] As you remember from the testosterone section of this chapter, higher forces have been shown to trigger testosterone responses while lighter ones have not.
- **Reduce fuel storage.** If you want to go those long distances, you need a big fuel tank, right? But when sprinting, you reach exhaustion fast, so you are sending a signal to the nervous system to reduce stored energy (meaning body

54 Jaquish, J., Singh, R., Hynote, E., & Conviser, J. (2012). Osteogenic Loading: A new modality to facilitate bone density development. Jaquish Industrial Research.

55 Heinonen, A., Kannus, P., Sievanen, H., Oja, P., Pasanen, M., Rinne, Ma., Uusi-Rasi, K., & Vuori, I. (1996). Randomised controlled trial of effect of high-impact exercise on selected risk factors for osteoporotic fractures. UKK Institute for Health Promotion Research. *Lancet* 1996; 348 (9038): 1343-1347.

56 Larson, P. (2019, June 13). Facts on Foot Strike. Retrieved from https://www.runnersworld.com/advanced/a20796790/facts-on-foot-strike/. *Runners World*.

fat) to allow you to become faster. As mentioned earlier in this chapter, stabilization firing drives this growth hormone induced reduction of body fat.

We call this the Sprint Effect, and much of it can be attributed to stabilization firing. As we've seen, research shows the key to upregulating hormone levels naturally is to apply heavy loads and high forces to the body while requiring it to stabilize itself under those loads. Research on sprinting confirms reflexive activation of muscle and muscle afferents is the triggering mechanism of the Sprint Effect.

MYOSTATIN

The MSTN gene provides instructions for making a protein called myostatin. This is an endogenous (created in the body) negative regulator of muscle growth that affects both muscle fiber number and size. In other words, its job is to keep you from growing muscle. It has become apparent over the past few years that animals with mutations stunting production of the myostatin protein experience incredible muscle growth.[57]

Here is an example of a cow that was a product of selected breeding intended to reduce myostatin levels with a resulting 30 percent greater ability to grow muscle. Keep in mind, nobody inspired this cow to start exercising. It just has almost no myostatin, and therefore grew more muscle.

57 Jespersen, J. G., Nedergaard, A., Andersen, L. L., Schjerling, P., & Andersen, J. L. (2011). Myostatin expression during human muscle hypertrophy and subsequent atrophy: increased myostatin with detraining. *Scandinavian Journal of Medicine & Science in Sports*, 21(2), 215-223.

Naturally, researchers studying the muscle-wasting dysfunctions associated with HIV and many types of cancer, as well as sports performance experts, became interested in how this protein might be downregulated to remove the associated limitations on muscular growth. Research performed with blood flow restriction techniques has already shown the potential to downregulate myostatin in multiple studies, producing muscle mass changes as well as added strength.[58,59]

Some researchers suggest blood flow restriction may make some of the body's skeletal muscle "invisible" for a period of time from a cardiac and/or nervous system perspective. The sudden "disappearance" of this "invisible" muscle might cause myostatin to be downregulated as the body makes an effort to return to homeostasis by growing replacement muscle. While the mechanisms are not well understood yet, the prospect of restricting myostatin to grow more muscle is worth pursuing as

58 Kawada, S. & Ishii, N. (2005). Skeletal muscle hypertrophy after chronic restriction of venous blood flow in rats. *Medicine and Science in Sports and Exercise*, *37*(7), 1144-1150.

59 Nielsen, J. L., Aagaard, P., Bech, R. D., Nygaard, T., Hvid, L. G., Wernbom, M., ... & Frandsen, U. (2012). Proliferation of myogenic stem cells in human skeletal muscle in response to low-load resistance training with blood flow restriction. *The Journal of Physiology*, 590(17), 4351-4361.

the existing studies on its downregulation have yielded promising outcomes for additional health benefits and muscularity.

So would using a blood flow restriction cuff like a tourniquet during exercise be an easy and effective way to downregulate myostatin? Not really. Research has shown the constrictive nature of blood flow restriction banding/tourniquets triggers neural inhibition—in other words, it begins to shut the muscle down, inhibiting your ability to achieve full muscle contraction. So while the cardiac signal for myostatin downregulation occurs during blood flow restriction, the associated neural inhibition negates this benefit by allowing for training with only a very light weight.[60,61] As we've learned, training light does not stimulate testosterone receptor activity or trigger testosterone creation. In addition, it would not contribute (or only minimally contribute) to up-regulating growth hormone since there is little need for stability firing when training with the nominal forces typical of blood flow restriction training, around 20 percent of one-rep maximum.[62]

The mechanism of myostatin downregulation triggered by restricting blood flow appears to be hypoxia, or a lower-than-normal concentration of oxygen in arterial blood. Hypoxia specifically has been shown to help subjects grow muscle mass

---

60 Netreba, AI, Popov, DV, Liubaeva, EV, Bravyi, I, Prostova, AB, Lemesheva, I, and Vinogradova, OL. (2007). Physiological effects of using the low intensity strength training without relaxation in single-joint and multi-joint movements. Ross. Fiziol. Zh. Im. I. M. Sechenova. 93: 27-38.

61 Netreba, AI, Popov, DV, Bravyi, I, Misina, SS, and Vinogradova, OL. (2009). Physiological effects of low-intensity strength training without relaxation. Fiziol. Cheloveka 35: 97-102.

62 Lixandrão, Manoel E., et al. "Effects of exercise intensity and occlusion pressure after 12 weeks of resistance training with blood-flow restriction." *European Journal of Applied Physiology* 115.12 (2015): 2471-2480.

even when users are forced to train with very light weights.[63] So what if we could get this restricted blood flow effect without using tourniquets, thereby combining the benefits of myostatin downregulation with the benefits of heavier loading on muscles?

In a recent *T-Nation* article, Brad Schoenfeld, PhD, an internationally renowned fitness expert, described an alternative way to create a hypoxic effect in target muscles by using constant tension throughout any given standard weightlifting movement. Many athletes simply refer to this as "constant tension." The authors state: "Repetitive muscular contractions cause a compression of blood vessels, impeding both inflow and outflow during exercise and creating a hypoxic intramuscular environment. There's evidence that the hypoxic effect mediates a hypertrophic response, conceivably by the buildup of metabolites and reduction in pH levels associated with such training."

In combination, these factors are believed to enhance muscular growth through various mechanisms including increased fiber recruitment, acute elevations in anabolic hormones, alterations in myokines, production of reactive oxygen species, and/or cell swelling (the pump)."[64] This was confirmed a year later in a study also pointing out the similarity in hypoxic effect to that achieved when training at altitude.[65,66] Contreras and Schoen-

63 Nishimura, A, Sugita, M, Kato, K, Fukuda, A, Sudo, A, and Uchida, A. Hypoxia increases muscle hypertrophy induced by resistance training. *Int. J. Sports Physiol. Perform.* 5: 497-508, 2010.

64 Contreras, B., & Schoenfeld, B. (2016, February 20). Tip: Use Continuous Tension for Muscle Gains. Retrieved January 14, 2020, from https://www.t-nation.com/training/tip-use-continuous-tension-for-muscle-gains.

65 Feriche, B., García-Ramos, A., Morales-Artacho, A. J., & Padial, P. (2017). Resistance training using different hypoxic training strategies: a basis for hypertrophy and muscle power development. *Sports Medicine-Open*, *3*(1), 12.

66 Moritani, T., Sherman, W. M., Shibata, M., Matsumoto, T., & Shinohara, M. (1992). Oxygen availability and motor unit activity in humans. *European Journal of Applied Physiology and Occupational Physiology*, 64(6), 552-556.

feld cited some serious limitations in attempting to train using constant tension with standard weights. "Some movements lead to a complete drop-off of joint torque and muscle activation in the targeted region. For example, the top of a chest fly or dumbbell pullover fails to place adequate tension on the targeted musculature."

CONCLUSIONS ABOUT HORMONES AND GROWTH FACTORS

Let's consider the results we've discussed so far and summarize the questions an ideal exercise program should answer:

- How do we get the maximum amount of hypoxia and associated myostatin downregulation without the biomechanical issues of maintaining constant tension in standard weightlifting?
- How do we achieve stability firing to create a far larger growth hormone effect with weights we couldn't normally lift due to the sticking point in the weaker range?
- How do we make the weights we work with heavier to trigger the maximum possible amount of testosterone upregulation as well as the greatest activity in testosterone receptors?

The answer to these questions is the key to maximizing muscle size, explosiveness, and strength—and even aggressive decreases in body fat—by upregulating muscle-building hormones, suppressing hormones designed to retain fat, activating stability firing, and using variable resistance to maximally stimulate the muscle in all ranges of motion.

And now that you have context, you'll appreciate exactly why we recommend exercising the way we do.

CHAPTER 4

INVENTING THE ULTIMATE SOLUTION FOR MAXIMIZING MUSCLE AND MINIMIZING BODY FAT

Now that we'd assembled a substantial portfolio of compelling scientific evidence proving variable resistance and hormonal stimulation were the keys to optimal muscle growth and fat loss, we were ready to see how our findings could be applied "in the field" when doing exercise. We already knew exactly how much variance was needed to elicit optimal muscular change based on John's newly plotted strength curve. Now we needed to determine the most effective way to deliver it. When looking at the strength curves, we knew there must be a simple and elegant solution, but it needed to apply to multiple movements, creating some design challenges:

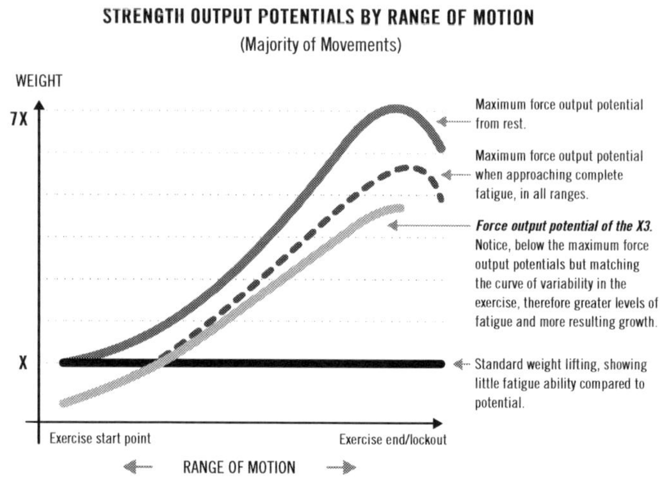

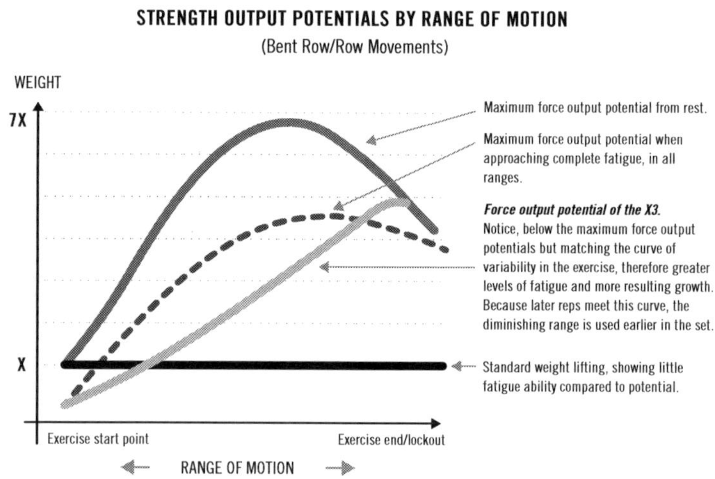

Because the resistance provided by elastic bands matches up fairly well against the desired force curve, John's first thought was to develop an exercise program using band training alone. But he soon found working out with just heavy bands was not practical. At the time strong bands were used primarily for pull-up assists by connecting the band to a pull-up bar and then hooking a foot through the band to help partially support body weight throughout the exercise. Unfortunately, when held directly in your hands or placed under your feet—for biceps curls or squats, for example—these can cause significant joint injury. While lighter bands didn't pose the same kind of risk, they also couldn't provide nearly adequate force to trigger real strength development. And if variable resistance doesn't deliver high peak forces in the strong range of motion, then its key advantage over ordinary weightlifting is eliminated, and possibly worse risk of injury is introduced.

Of course, this hasn't stopped a few elastic (some petroleum-based rubber, some higher quality latex) band sellers from attempting to market bands alone as the ideal training method. But people have been making that claim for decades, and band-only training hasn't superseded weight training at all. No doubt many who tried band-only training at high force levels learned firsthand this is a practical impossibility for the reasons mentioned above. People who think you can safely perform exercises with multi-hundred-pound bands in isolation have never tried it. Or they're really just hucksters trying to create market confusion. To make a weightlifting analogy, nobody is discarding the barbell and just hanging a bunch of iron plates on their fingers to do a bench press.

For clarification, here are two examples of how heavy bands twist small joints in a way that induces neural inhibition and prevents them from being a useful training tool, and could potentially cause permanent injury.

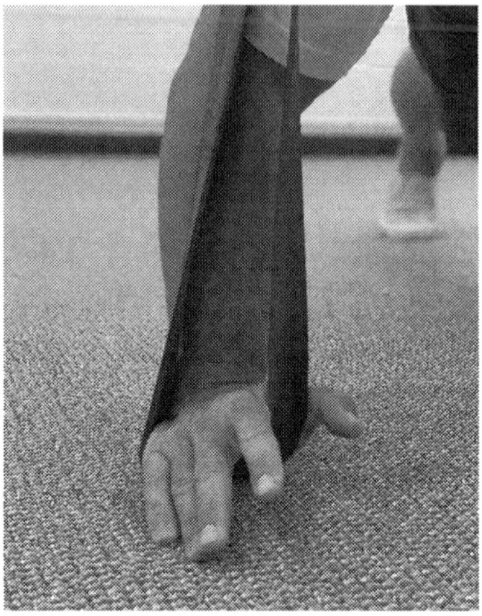 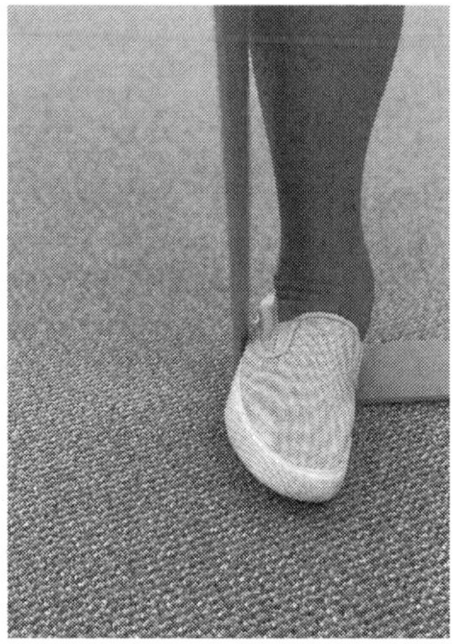

At least now we knew why everyone hadn't already moved from weights to training with heavy bands. It wasn't a problem with variable resistance. It was simply the case that a practical way for exercises to handle high forces while using bands didn't exist yet. It was time to develop something amazing.

CONCEIVING AND DESIGNING X3

John once again took an approach taught to him by his inventor father and set to work on developing a safer and more effective way to train with bands. He was looking for a solution capitalizing on the strength levels he'd quantified in his OsteoStrong research, something far more powerful than conventional exercise bands or weightlifting. This time, he envisioned incorporating an Olympic-style barbell, a second ground to stand on, and interchangeable bands providing varying levels of resistance with peak forces FAR beyond what could be achieved with standard weight training. John made a cocktail napkin drawing of his idea and emailed it to Henry.

Still a Cal Poly college student at the time, Henry interpreted John's sketch to be a bar with self-tightening clamps at the end so users wouldn't have to worry about the band slipping out as the workout progressed. He ran with the idea, creating a 3D CAD model. Admittedly, the result was pretty odd-looking.

It also wasn't at all what John had envisioned. Henry recalls John asking him, "What the hell is this?" They cleared up the misinterpretation and kept working.

The next iteration looked a lot more like the finished product we have today. Henry designed the bar with hooks for the bands to attach to safely. Internal bearings moved the bar with the user's hand throughout the range of motion, maximizing force production and protecting the wrists from injury. The ground plate created both a stable surface to stand on and a place the bands could move freely under, preventing the ankles from turning inward.

WHY AN OLYMPIC STYLE BARBELL?

People often ask us why we chose to incorporate a bar rather than two unconnected handles when designing X3. The answer is peak force. Using a barbell maximizes the amount of force you can produce and withstand. As we've discussed in previous chapters, this is key to stimulating the right hormones for fat loss and muscle growth.

John recently discussed competitive weightlifting with sports performance documentary maker Chris Bell, writer and director of *Bigger, Stronger, Faster* (2008). Chris and his brother Mark have been competitive lifters most of their lives, and Chris covers strength industry news on his podcast and social media outlets. So when John asked Chris, "What do the strongest people in the world train with—barbells or dumbbells?" Chris replied, "Barbells!"

When John asked why, Chris explained that it's a matter of practicality and what's most effective. As humans, we pick up heavy objects symmetrically using both hands and legs. If you had a heavy object to move, you'd grab it with both arms, right? THAT is functional. Nobody would put one hand in their pocket and attempt the task with the other.

This is the same way the central nervous system sees exercise. Two-armed exercises activate more muscle because your arms are designed to work together. In 2011, researchers observed subjects could lift close to 20 percent more weight with the barbell bench press as opposed to the dumbbell press. In 2012, further research demonstrated a 10 percent greater force production capacity for barbells in standing overhead pressing.[67] This was echoed in 2012 with another group of researchers.[68] Chris intuitively knew what the research had also proven, based on his experience watching some of the strongest people in the world train for years.

So what are the mechanisms involved in this process? Why can't we lift more with our hands independently or during activities like dumbbell presses? As we've already noted, you wouldn't pick up something heavy with one hand. You also wouldn't pick up two heavy things and balance one in each hand in the

67 Stock, M. S., Beck, T. W., DeFreitas, J. M., & Dillon, M. A. (2011). Test–retest reliability of barbell velocity during the free-weight bench-press exercise. *The Journal of Strength & Conditioning Research*, 25(1), 171-177.

68 Saeterbakken, A. H., & Fimland, M. S. (2012). Muscle activity of the core during bilateral, unilateral, seated and standing resistance exercise. *European Journal of Applied Physiology*, 112(5), 1671-1678.

course of daily living, and neither would your ancestors. It's just not going to happen, and thus it's not something the human body evolved to do. For this reason, the central nervous system doesn't process these movements as something the human body does, and therefore cannot respond in an effective manner. Other physiological mechanisms aside, it's clear the weight we can handle using our limbs independently is much lower than when using them together, and lower exercise forces eliminate many opportunities for growth.

The strongest people in the world use barbells, not dumbbells. Yes, we know the World's Strongest Man contest features an event to see how high contestants can throw a fifty-pound dumbbell in the air. But that's a contest...it's NOT how the participants actually built their strength and muscularity.

MATERIALS SELECTION

Most Olympic bars are made out of regular steel—not the stainless kind—and then plated with nickel, zinc, or chrome. If you look at older barbells in a gym, they're generally rusted because the steel underneath has been exposed as plating wore off through repeated use. We wanted X3 to be resistant to that kind of corrosion. We also wanted the Olympic barbell to be relatively light, so we decided to make the outer tube of the X3 bar out of aluminum. We anodized it to create a hard, attractive coating that does not rust or discolor. There's a reason Apple makes so many products with this same material and surface treatment—it offers an attractive, consistent finish. Given the profound effect this device has on its user, we wanted to make sure it had as impressive a visual effect as its physiological effect—even if that meant using more expensive materials than most fitness companies use in their products.

While stainless steel would have been too heavy for the actual bar, we used it to make hooks that hold the bands on to the X3. There's no concern about extra weight here because it's a smaller component requiring less volume of material. As an external part, being rust-resistant is an important benefit.

The interior of the bar is a cold-rolled steel shaft. As the major load-bearing component of X3 interfacing directly with the hooks and bearings and any torque applied to them, we wanted to ensure it was strong enough to handle peak forces. Inside the shaft are bearings that enable the bar to move in the user's hands throughout the range of motion. This allows for maximum force production. If the hooks were fixed, the bar would twist your wrists—creating an unnatural angle, potentially causing injury, and limiting loading. Anything that limits loading also limits workout efficacy.

The bearings themselves are made of self-lubricating nylon. They move at slow speeds designed to match the controlled manner in which X3 exercises are done. For X3 purposes, nylon bearings are superior to needle bearings or bronze bushings. Needle bearings are made out of steel, require external lubrication to function properly, and have the potential to rust, corrode, or become gummy and stiff if they are infiltrated by dirt or dust. Bronze bushings also require external lubrication to minimize friction, and oil-impregnated bronze bushings rely on high rotational speeds to draw lubricant out of the bearing itself (the X3 would never be subject to this type of continuous high-speed rotation). In contrast, nylon requires no maintenance or external lubricants, will not corrode, does not involve a complex mechanism that could be jammed with dust or dirt, and does not benefit from high-speed rotation.

We chose all the materials for the X3 bar with strength, superiority, durability, and safety in mind. There are always people who will say, "I can just get a wooden stick and do this." Then they attach bands to a broomstick, it breaks, and they get hurt. In the same vein, we wanted to avoid injury by making sure the bar couldn't be changed or retrofitted, so we designed it to be both durable and difficult to disassemble.

BAR SIZING

The X3 bar is nineteen inches wide. Biomechanical and human size data shows more than 95 percent of the population fits within this range in terms of shoulder width.[69] Some people fear nineteen inches won't provide enough length to get the workout they want. These are usually bodybuilders who like doing wide-grip chest presses because they can handle more weight that way. However, from a workout perspective, the added pounds only reflect adopting a position of superior mechanical leverage on the bar that actually promotes an *inferior* pectoral contraction.

Clearly, if you want to achieve optimal muscle growth, a wide-grip chest press is not the way to achieve your goals. Think about it: where are your pectorals more contracted—when your arms are wide, or when you are pushing them directly away from your body and the backs of your hands are in line with the shoulder joints? The positioning of the hands on our nineteen-inch Olympic bar produces more pectoral stimulation and muscle contraction. Since the objective of X3 is to make people as strong as possible, we designed the bar's proportions to ensure users are doing the most effective workout possible.

---

69 McDowell, M. A., Fryar, C. D., & Ogden, C. L. (2009). Anthropometric reference data for children and adults: United States, 1988-1994. *Vital and health statistics. Series 11, Data from the national health survey*, (249), 1-68.

EXPERIMENTING WITH THE BANDS

Next, we went in search of the strongest, most durable bands in the world. The goal was to find the bands that produced the greatest amount of force and got as close as possible to the strength curves we'd plotted through our research with OsteoStrong.

We started by testing physical therapy bands. Physical therapists already understand the principles of variable resistance and its ability to enhance exercise safety, typically using bands to help rehabilitate small joint dysfunctions for this reason. However, it quickly became clear PT bands could not provide enough resistance. They're intentionally light to provide therapeutic injury treatment. As we've discussed in earlier chapters, you need heavier loads to build muscle.

We then bought and tested a wide variety of bands from virtually every manufacturer we could find. Some were terrible, stretching out and getting longer every time we'd use them. Some bands barely stretched at all and therefore couldn't be used to perform any exercises. Yet other products were even lower resistance than the bands sold into the therapy market. These low performers were the typical $10 bands you can buy from the big box stores. It was laughable, and we wondered to what extent they were to blame for variable-resistance training's lack of popularity in the fitness world.

The bands we tested also had a wide price disparity. Some were more than $100 for a single band while other entire sets cost only $20. It became clear there was a big difference in the quality of these products.

Speaking with a material science engineer who'd worked with

technology-forward companies like Tesla and Apple helped us hone down our choices. In particular, the engineer suggested focusing our band trials on those made of latex rather than petroleum. While petroleum stretches out, latex keeps its length and can provide more power per unit volume of material.

Eventually, we winnowed down the remaining contenders to a small group that offered the greatest power available. Among those, we conducted further testing to see which band provided the absolute best variance and resistance. We were looking for one that could stretch through the entire range of motion, significantly increase force production throughout as it was stretched, and still not become so taut it was impossible to use.

The winner was a band type of our own design, consisting of thirty layers of latex. When compared to typical latex banding of the same width, ours offers more than 33 percent the depth and delivers more power than any bands we could find on the market. Layered bands are strong, provide the appropriate amount of resistance, and do not stretch out. The layering also provides a built-in safety feature, making the bands highly resistant to dangerous breakage. Bands made without this process are potentially composed of only one layer, and if it were to potentially snap there would be no additional layers to fall back on. The resultant failure would present an additional risk of injuring users.

Our banding is made with latex sourced from trees in Sri Lanka, and our manufacturer there is the only one we've identified that can produce bands of this quality and endurance.

We are aware that one percent of the population has a latex allergy—in fact, John is part of that one percent. If you are too, rest assured you can still work out with X3. In this case, our advice is to avoid skin-to-skin contact with the band by wearing a shirt while working out and then showering afterwards. In other words, do what you'd normally do during and after exercise.

STABILIZATION THROUGH THE GROUND PLATE

The small joints in our bodies, specifically wrists and ankles, interface well with flat surfaces. They don't do well with round surfaces. When joints get twisted, they get injured. In addition, as discussed in chapter three, stabilization is a key factor in stimulating hormonal release.

With that in mind, we knew we needed to create a plate component for the X3 so the user wouldn't have to stand on the band during whole-body exercises. This plate functions like a second ground. The band travels underneath the plate inside a channel while the user stands on the plate, thereby protecting the ankles from being rotated inward by the extremely high forces encountered during some exercises. In this way, the plate allows you to enjoy the full benefit of high force variable-resistance training.

To put this in context, we recently measured John producing more than 640 pounds of peak force during deadlift testing. The ground plate obviously served an important role in protecting his ankles from being twisted inwards by this movement—otherwise, that 640 pounds could have easily triggered enough neural inhibition to prevent him from completing the lift, or worse, potentially broken some small bones in the ankle joint.

THE X3 PROTOTYPE IS BORN

Now that we had a prototype in hand, we were excited to begin using it and seeing the results of all our research and development. Combining the best parts of weightlifting—using an Olympic style barbell while standing on a flat ground surface—and variable resistance, by adding highly variable, heavy-duty elastic bands, we knew in theory X3 should offer the most efficient, effective delivery of force throughout the entire range of motion.

Had we finally invented a variable-resistance device that could deliver force closest to the curve of human force production? Could it really stimulate optimal hormonal release, fat loss, and muscle growth for a faster, better workout than anything else available in the fitness world?

It was time to find out.

CHAPTER 5

X3 IN ACTION

During X3's testing period, John was busy traveling the world speaking about bone density and OsteoStrong. Though X3 wasn't designed to be a travel tool, it did fit nicely into his checked bag, so he decided to keep the prototype with him at all times.

As fellow frequent business travelers know all too well, it can be hard to stay on track nutritionally while on the road. At some airports, especially in Europe, it seems like beer, chocolate, and pastries are the only options. Since how and when we eat is just as important—if not more so—than fitness routines, John was not expecting optimal results.

But when John returned from an extended European speaking tour, Henry was astounded by the changes he saw in his friend. "Well, X3 is clearly working," was Henry's comment when John walked into the office. It was quite an understatement, despite all the terrible airport food.

JOHN'S PERSONAL EXPERIENCE

I was scrawny as a kid, and I hated it. When I was fourteen years old, a girl I liked said she didn't want to go out with me because I was too skinny. The first thing I did when I got my driver's license was start going to the gym.

After I began lifting weights, I was frustrated by any lack of significant growth response. The older guys I looked up to at the gym never seemed to change much physically either. I could tell they developed some muscle at some point, but they were just going in day after day, year after year, with no further changes.

I realized whatever the answer to muscle growth was, it was not in that building. I also came to a slightly different conclusion than many people did when looking at the trend of people signing up for the gym, and then never going, and then quitting maybe a year or two later. Many people cite laziness as the reason that others don't commit themselves to the gym, but I would argue that the real reason might have to do with the gym's lack of efficacy. I'd say that when people know they can get what they really want, they aren't lazy. They go for it.

For example, almost everyone in Westernized countries has an expensive smartphone, even if it costs twice their monthly rent or mortgage. People on social welfare even seem to find a way to pay for their smartphones. Why? When people want something badly enough, they find a way. So even back then, I didn't think people who quit the gym were lazy. I thought they were people who gave it an honest try and saw almost no results—or no results at all.

I wrestled, swam, and ran track (athletics if you are reading this in the UK) in high school. When I went to college, I wanted to try a different sport. I was six feet tall and an extremely lean 140 pounds at the time, so I wanted to get involved with something that encouraged a greater level of strength and size.

I went out for the rugby team. After five years as an undergrad (yeah, I took a victory lap, which was highly encouraged by my fraternity), I ended up at 160 pounds. I had gained a little more strength than when I arrived on campus, but I had definitely lost my visible abdominals. In retrospect, I really didn't progress much during those years in terms of strength or muscle gains.

In the subsequent fifteen years, I gained maybe a few pounds of muscle. And then at twenty-eight years old, I was prescribed testosterone replacement therapy (TRT). This is young to begin TRT, but my levels were so low they meant I was at high risk for a cardiac incident. This was as a result of a rugby injury I didn't think much of at the time, but it was actually a big deal.

Many myths about this therapy exist on the internet. I even did an episode on *The Falsehoods of Fitness* on my YouTube channel about how TRT is not an advantage, it's just replacing something naturally meant to be there but that is missing. Because I was so low in testosterone before starting the therapy, I put on a few pounds of muscle after starting it. But because the TRT only replaced the testosterone I was missing hormonally and remained at a natural level, nothing dramatic happened. This is the case with almost all TRT patients.

I kept strength training, but I felt my joints becoming irritated. I wasn't like some lifters who simply push through the pain—I knew this was the point to *stop* pushing because otherwise I would injure myself. And the London research had shown there were physiological limitations to standard weightlifting

I wouldn't be able to overcome no matter how hard I trained. Luckily, I now knew how to circumvent these.

JOHN'S STATS BEFORE THE X3 PROTOTYPE

By this point, I had been lifting weights for twenty years. I still stood six feet tall, was now 190 pounds, and had 20 percent body fat. I thought those were some lousy results (and I was pretty self-conscious about it), but I imagined I simply didn't have the genetics to do much better. I also felt like every time I tried to restrict calories, I lost muscle, and every time I tried to add mass through calorie surplus, I just put on fat. At times I wondered if I'd reached some sort of personal physical limit.

Once we had the X3 prototype, I was more than excited to test its efficacy. My biggest hope was that it would help me break out of the place I'd been stuck for so long. Happily, I began changing by the day once I started using it. Obviously, the barrier to achieving the physique I wanted all along hadn't been supplements or nutrition, but stimulation for growth. At the end of the first year using X3, I went from 190 pounds and 20 percent body fat to 205 pounds and 11 percent body fat. That means that in a single year, I gained thirty pounds of muscle and lost sixteen pounds of body fat.

And the results didn't stop there. Within the first two years of training with X3, I'd put on forty-five pounds of muscle and lost nearly twenty pounds of body fat—and my stats are continually improving to this day. I just keep getting leaner; I continue to replace fat with muscle. Recent DEXA scans (Dual Energy X-ray Absorptiometry, the best way to understand body composition by analyzing fat, muscle, bone, and tissues individually) confirm this fact.

Lean body mass, (LBM)

Day One

190 pounds
20 percent body fat
152 LBM with 38 pounds of fat

End of Year One

205 pounds
11 percent body fat
183 LBM with 22 pounds of fat

End of Year Two

220 pounds
9 percent body fat
198 LBM with 22 pounds of fat
NET LEAN MASS GAIN: 45 pounds
NET FAT LOSS: 16 pounds

I assumed my results might eventually level out, but I'm going much further than I ever thought I could. A few days ago, I broke all my records standing right next to Henry in our office. Here's something most forty-three-year-old guys can't claim but I can: with X3, I just keep getting stronger.

Many people think you aren't able to significantly change your physique once you hit a certain age. They believe a twenty-one-year-old person who's out of shape can achieve big results by just following an exercise and diet protocol. But if someone in their thirties or beyond did the same, their changes wouldn't be nearly as noticeable—if any changes even occur at all.

I'd challenge that notion. I was over forty when I started training with X3. My impressive physical transformation came from this invention alone. The scientific principles it capitalizes on to create visible changes work regardless of age.

Just as a side note and possible metaphor for the growth/healthy development of many different types of human tissue: my first invention, OsteoStrong medical devices, allows elderly deconditioned women to grow bone density just as fast as men who are athletic and in their twenties. Many perceived physical limitations relating to poor conditioning later in life may relate more to a poor strategy for stimulating development than actual limitations. Both of my inventions and their results with consumers support this.

HENRY'S PERSONAL EXPERIENCE

Once I saw how John's body had changed using X3, I asked him to make another prototype for my own use. In college, I had done regular strength training, spending hours at the gym every week, so I was eager to see how that experience would compare with using X3.

Since bulking up wasn't my main focus, I didn't follow John's X3 training regimen closely. While John represents a prime example of the results that can be achieved by carefully and consistently following the X3 protocol that is now recommended to customers, I was more casual about my training. I used X3 several times a week and cherry-picked which exercises to do on any given day.

Even so, I put on ten pounds of muscle that year. For all the hours I logged at the gym during college, I saw no significant changes to my physique. But by training with X3 for about ten minutes a day, several times a week, I successfully added measurable increases to both my muscle mass and definition. My girlfriend even noticed that it improved how my shirts and work clothes fit.

I strongly believe I could push my results a lot farther if I wanted to, but I'm happy working out this way. I get a lot more out of X3 than I ever did with weightlifting, in far less time, which is a crucial benefit.

The benefits didn't stop there. I hadn't been cycling as much as I normally would due to work obligations, but I recently went for a ride with a friend. We decided to bike Mount Diablo, a twenty-nine-mile ride climbing four thousand feet with an eight out of ten difficulty rating. Not only did I ride the entire way without having to stop and recover, but I felt strong throughout. I even passed riders on the way up! Since I wasn't doing any other exercise during the preceding multi-month hiatus from cycling, I credit X3 for my ability to ride much more strongly than I would have expected. In fact, I'm not sure my performance would have been much better if I followed a more consistent training regimen that actually involved cycling. This result was quite unexpected to me at the time, but as I learned later, it is actually consistent with research on the aerobic benefits of exercise like X3, which is discussed at length later in this book.

MOVING FORWARD WITH X3

Knowing Henry's main fitness passion was cycling, John saw his friend's enthusiasm as confirmation of X3's wide appeal. Its results would excite anyone who wanted to be in shape for a particular sport, event, or just life in general.

X3 was for everyone.

Our personal experience with X3 provided further proof that variable-resistance training using peak force throughout the ranges of motion was vastly superior to weight training. It also demonstrated how well X3 leveraged our variable-resistance and hormonal research and findings into a practical, simple, fast, portable training solution.

In the face of conventional fitness "wisdom" that espouses calorie burn for weight loss, people may wonder how we could do a ten-minute workout yet still lose weight and gain muscle. The hormonal effect provided by X3 answers that question.

X3 combines the self-stabilizing, natural multi-joint movements used in weight training with the higher forces provided by the variable resistance. No longer limited to the weak range of motion, these higher forces activate greater stabilization firing and thus X3 presumably stimulates even more release of growth hormone than would be possible with fixed weights. Because it enables heavier training with more repetitions, testosterone is also triggered. Stabilization adds a greater total muscular stimulus and creates a deeper level of fatigue. Translation: X3 enables users to lose body fat, maintain muscle mass, and build muscle all at the same time.

What's more, delivering variable resistance in high ratios and keeping constant tension throughout each exercise allows X3 to create a hypoxic effect on muscles. This promotes myostatin downregulation and contributes to an even greater muscle mass growth effect. (You can find the specific X3 protocol we developed and how to apply this information to transform your body composition in this book's appendix.)

In our meta-analysis, we hypothesized the key to upregulating growth hormone levels naturally is the application of heavy loads and high forces while in a circumstance where the body is required to self-stabilize. To achieve those parameters, you need a free movement exercise system like X3, not a machine. Working out with X3 produced results consistent with our hypothesis on this subject.

It's important to note we published our meta-analysis before inventing X3. This type of research represents the highest level of unbiased medical evidence. It utilizes independent studies conducted without our involvement and before our product was even in existence.

Like we've stated before, our intention was never to get into the fitness sector. We're biomedical engineers, and our professional experience is in the medical field. But based on our research and personal experiences, we truly believed X3 was going to be a game-changer in terms of how people exercise. So even though we were initially hesitant to get into the fitness space, it was like we *had* to. X3 was the absolute, ultimate fitness device.

SOURCING AND MANUFACTURING

Once we decided to proceed with making X3 available to the public, we needed to find a way to manufacture it in an effective manner. This was an interesting challenge because we needed to start with very small production runs, which are expensive and unappealing to vendors. But we also needed to build a supply chain with the ultimate goal of scaling to produce as many units as we would eventually be able to sell—which we hoped and expected would be a lot of X3s.

Other than the bands, which are made in Sri Lanka, all the parts for the X3 are sourced in America. The major bar components come from Nevada City, California, where we're headquartered. Other parts of the product have been sourced from Connecticut, Illinois, Tennessee, and Florida.

Parts generally pass through our headquarters in Nevada City as a function of our quality assurance efforts. A moving service then picks up approved parts on pallets from our facility and brings them to Sacramento, where bar and ground plate assembly occurs. Occasionally, we have pitched in at the Sacramento facility during the normal staff's off-hours to build additional X3s and help increase the production rate. That means some current X3 customers actually own systems that were handmade by its inventors.

Assembled bars and ground plates are then shipped to Knoxville, Tennessee, or Salt Lake City. This is where they meet up with the bands, which have been shipped there from Sri Lanka. All components are packaged, boxed, and shipped from one of those two warehouse locations.

We're proud that our invention has helped create jobs in the U.S. One of our main vendors in Nevada City actually had to move to a building three times their former size based on our business. They are now in the process of expanding into the neighboring building, which will roughly double their current size once the move is complete. They have more than quadrupled their staff because of X3. We love our country, and we know one way to make it better is by creating new jobs for our fellow Americans.

MAKER TURNS MODEL

Although we considered hiring a spokesperson to be the face of our new product, we identified several challenges with this approach. One was that the public might not believe our chosen representative looked the way they did due to X3 exclusively, or even in part. We understood the objection; clearly, anyone we picked would be in good shape even before they started using our product.

Another concern was that such a person might choose to continue other training elements beyond just X3—say, still weightlifting or running—during their tenure. After all, athletes and fitness professionals have been training in conventional ways for years by the time they have any noticeable level of physical change in the body. It would be hard for them to completely forsake these habits for something new and different, and if they kept using old training methods it would undermine the message of our educational campaign. Plus, people might simply think our spokesperson was only touting X3 as the next revolution in fitness because we were paying them to say that.

Finally, we hadn't written this book yet. Distilling the years of research that went into developing X3 would be difficult without a guide like this, and it wasn't fair to expect the person we chose to be able to explain all the concepts behind our product's efficacy. If we had been able to consolidate and explain all that science easily, we might have gone a different route. But as you can see from the many citations lining the bottom of almost every page here, the studies X3 is based on are complicated and multitudinous.

In the end, John reluctantly decided to step up to the plate. He'd been waiting for something as effective at building muscle as X3 for decades. When the prototype started giving him the physique he'd always wanted, he realized he should document the changes to his body to help people understand the results X3 delivers. So while we were filing for the patent in sixty-six countries, John started taking frequent pictures of himself, many of which we still use on our website, social media, and packaging today.

John says, "I hated being the guy in the pictures in the beginning. I made myself a fitness model for the product when I was at 20 percent body fat. I did not look good. Fortunately, my conditioning changed quickly, and the people who had been following from the beginning noticed. Even now people comment on how they find an earlier training video on YouTube and can't believe the difference.

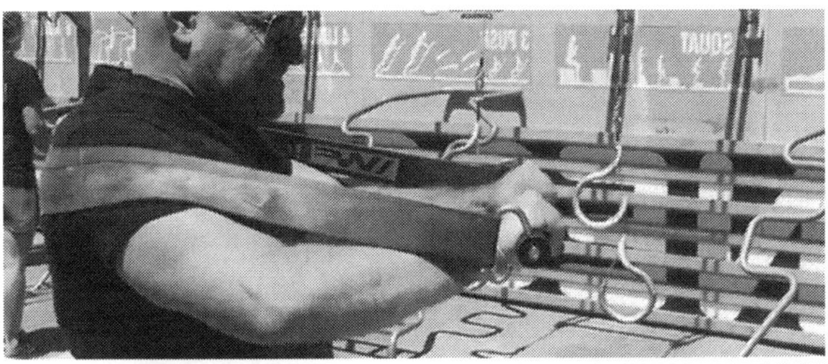

Although you might have thought John looked strong prior to starting X3 training, his body underwent a major transformation after he started using it. He put on muscle and lost fat at the same time, which many people mistakenly believe is physiologically impossible, in large part because they don't understand the role of hormones, growth factors, and variable resistance, as discussed in earlier chapters.

What's more, we can confirm without a doubt his results are one hundred percent due to our invention.

EARLY X3 ADOPTERS

Soon, we went out on pre-order with a superior, high-quality, made in the USA product. We marketed it direct to consumer through our website and social media advertising.

We also did a soft launch on Dave Asprey's podcast, *Bulletproof Radio*. Dave is famous for creating Bulletproof coffee—the kind that includes butter and MCT oil—and his never-ending quest for the ultimate way to biohack his body and mind. He was the first person outside the company to receive an X3 and liked the results he was getting from it so much he invited John to be on the podcast.

As a result of John's appearance on Dave's podcast as well as some other top health podcasts, X3 experienced an instant boost in sales. Even though we were staging an industry disruption by going against everything people supposedly "knew" about fitness, many *Bulletproof* devotees were willing to try X3. Although we were saying something no one else was saying, the scientific proof was irrefutable.

Dave made a few videos about his results. Shortly after that,

Ben Greenfield had John on his podcast as well as *SuperHuman Radio*. John was also invited to be on Ben Pakulski's podcast *International Federation of Body Building (IFBB) Pro*.

CURRENT X3 USERS

John used X3 to develop his musculature as much as possible. Henry used it to enhance his cycling. Dave Asprey confirmed it as an effective biohack. Once the product was available to the general population, it became clear that this was just the beginning. There are as many satisfied X3 users as there are uses for the X3 system. The following is just a brief sampling of the wide variety of people who have incorporated X3 into their workouts.

PROFESSIONAL ATHLETES

Team owners and athletes are sensitive about their brands. Because we don't sponsor or pay money for any of the following to endorse our products, in most cases we can't name names. However, we can give you a general idea of the pros turning to X3 for time-efficient, muscle-building workouts, such as:

- Forrest Griffin. A former light heavyweight champion of mixed martial arts (MMA), one of the best fighters of all time, uses X3 exclusively. He suffers from joint injuries, and X3 has made it possible for him to work out hard again.
- Well-known, recently retired professional athletes in football and basketball use X3 to stay in shape now that they are no longer playing their sport.
- A professional basketball team in Florida has been using X3 for over a year to increase their fitness and strength on the court. Their conditioning coaches reached out to us to

implement X3 as a training protocol after hearing John on the *Ben Greenfield Fitness* podcast.

- A well-known twenty-year quarterback from New England has posted videos of himself using X3 on social media. He often attributes high performance at his age to not using weights, which he has always disliked because of potential joint damage. Word has it his other Boston-based teammates use X3 as well.
- A group of professional swimmers out of Los Angeles have been using X3 for over a year as the land training component of their workouts. One of these athletes is currently featured on our website and is in training for the Para-Olympics.

BODYBUILDERS

Phil Hernon, Mr. USA 1996, was one of our earliest adopters. After explaining to him how X3 worked scientifically, he decided to give it a try. After using it for just a few weeks, he declared, "I'm never going to the gym again." He makes an appearance in our original X3 advertisement and now uses X3 exclusively.

Phil now serves as trainer to Gadiel Micu, Mr. USA 1992. Gadiel is a fifty-six-year-old California Corrections Officer who had stopped training for a number of years. Two years ago, he began training again with X3 exclusively. At the 2019 Central California Bodybuilding Championships, he won first place in three categories: Lightweight Men's Open Bodybuilding, overall Men's Bodybuilding Over 50s, and Overall Classic Men's Physique Over 40s. The open class victory is particularly telling, as it means he beat competitors of all age categories, including those in their twenties.

An Olympic lifter reported to us that he got more results from six months of X3 than he did out of twenty years of lifting weights. The bodybuilders of Generation Iron are also fans of X3.

FITNESS AND NUTRITION LEADERS

Dr. Shawn Baker is the leading authority on carnivore nutrition and host of the podcast *Human Performance Outliers*. While we do sponsor his show, he is a true proponent of X3. He reports X3 is the hardest workout he's ever done.

As he says, "X3 is no joke. It will wipe you out. If you are not motivated to do a really hard strength workout, X3 is not for you."

MEDICAL PROFESSIONALS

Based on our observations of the Facebook X3 Users Group page, doctors and physical therapists comprised a large portion of our earliest adopters. We even saw a few MD-PhDs! Medical doctors don't usually endorse weightlifting as they see so many injuries related to it, but they quickly understood the benefits of X3.

On this subject, when we first started out, internet trolls implied we were trying to trick people into buying X3 with made-up science. We hardly think a customer base as scientifically literate, well educated, and highly researched as ours would fall prey to such false claims. Our website (and this book) currently includes multiple testimonials from MDs, and the scientific studies we refer to are properly cited in all our materials for anyone who wants to review them and assess the evidence for themselves.

THE MILITARY

As with the pro athletes, we are unable to specifically name our military users. However, we can confirm that several elite units are incorporating X3 into their training regimens.

We've also observed in the Facebook Users Group that X3 not only makes working out when deployed easier and more effective, but that users have also exceeded performance standards and previous records on military tests after training with X3.

CROSSFIT COMPETITORS

We've spoken with CrossFit competitors who train exclusively with X3 yet continue to win contests because of the added strength it gives them. Imagine no more "workouts of the day" (WODs) or driving to the box to work out and still crushing the competition.

X3 CUSTOMER STORIES

Some customers have shared their personal X3 experiences with us at great length. With their permission, we have included a few of them here. In this way, you can see how our experience compares with that of people from a variety of different backgrounds who were not involved with creating the product.

The stories that follow are from relatively early adopters of X3 who were not new to strength training. They all achieved the best results we could have hoped for, and that they have ever experienced. We see similar results with an enormous number of customers, and for us, that provides some real-world validation to our scientific hypotheses.

We don't want to distract from the science presented in the book. We believe these benefits would be shown in a randomized, controlled trial, and are currently discussing that possibility with several universities. But for now, we can only draw from the evidence available to us, and we think that case studies of our customers tell a compelling story.

JASON YOUNG

Quick Stats: A quintessential hard-gainer who had exercised for decades, Jason Young lost a pound of fat and gained thirty-five pounds of muscle after switching to X3. He is forty-seven years old at the time of this writing and considers himself to be in **the best shape of his life.**

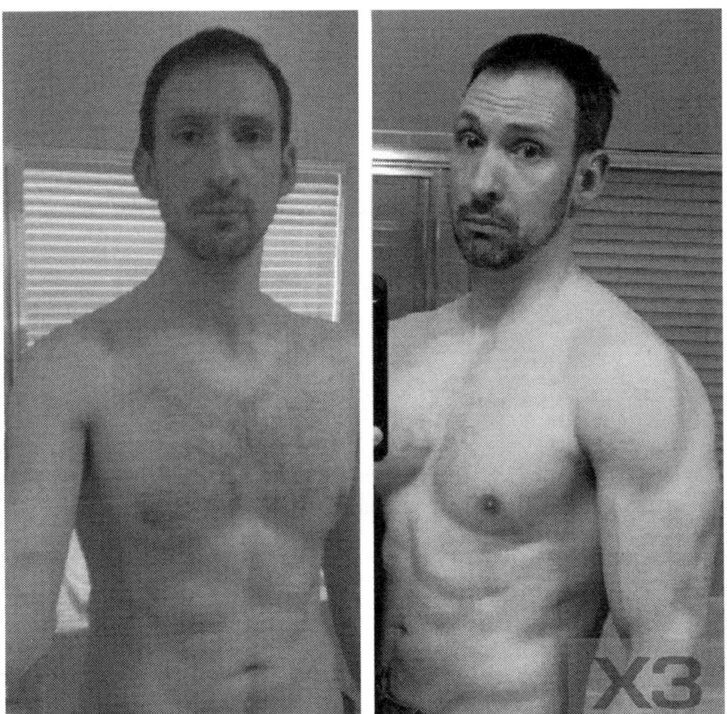

Jason Young was in and out of the fitness scene for nearly thirty years after joining the Army at eighteen. Despite his lifelong commitment to exercise, Young describes himself as a quintessential hard-gainer. At five-foot-eleven, his weight typically hovered around 150 pounds. At the very height of his lifting routine, he tipped the scales at about 200 pounds, but the great gains came at a price.

Heavy lifting took its toll, and Young frequently suffered joint pain and other weightlifting-related injuries which would set him back again and again, sometimes for months. Eventually, he fell into a five-year slump, dropping back down to his typical body weight and losing much of his athletic physique. Young describes his mindset at the end of those five years: "Early last year, I saw the beginnings of a transformation taking place on me...skinny-fat dad-bod. I was kind of horrified. It was enough of a wake-up call to motivate me to start exercising again. I decided I needed to find an exercise regimen with minimal joint stress and injury risk. I wanted to do something I could perform into old age."

With this in mind, Young committed himself to a training regimen using some of the lightweight tube bands that are on the market, and for a short while things were going great. After a couple of months, Young noticed that he was again experiencing joint pain, but of a different variety than he experienced when lifting heavy weights. "I knew it was due to the angular forces being imposed on my joints by the bands, and I began searching for something to relieve those forces and spare my joints. This is when X3 ads started showing up. I was intrigued. I read all I could find about it and decided to make the purchase." Young went all-in on X3 and has been committed to the workouts for fifteen months now. Since then he's put on thirty-five pounds of lean body mass and maintains that he's currently in the best shape of his life at the age of forty-seven.

Though he's dealt with a number of setbacks in the last year—all prior injuries from his heavy lifting days—he says these gave him an even greater appreciation of the X3 system and programming. Young was able to use the X3 to rehab outstanding injuries, as well as maintain an exercise regimen and continue to make gains. "Unfortunately, I suffer from a debilitating case of CLS (Chicken Leg Syndrome). I've seen more leg development with X3 than anything else I've ever tried. Before, I'd always end up having to back off leg exercises because they would aggravate an old knee injury. With X3 I've gotten further than I have with any other training protocol."

Young makes it clear his great results with X3 aren't from minimal effort. "It takes a lot of mental discipline and focus to work muscles to complete fatigue using this modality. When folks understand that getting desired results is about efficiently stimulating the CNS to trigger growth, they'll really appreciate the effectiveness of the X3 and the programming. The slow cadence reps are soul-crushing, and it takes me several minutes to recover between sets, but the results are well worth it!"

JOHN FERRO

Quick Stats: In just over one year, John lost twenty-two pounds of fat and gained eight pounds of muscle using X3. John has managed this despite largely flouting the X3 nutrition guidelines (discussed later in this book) and he often posts pictures of pizza on the X3 online forum.

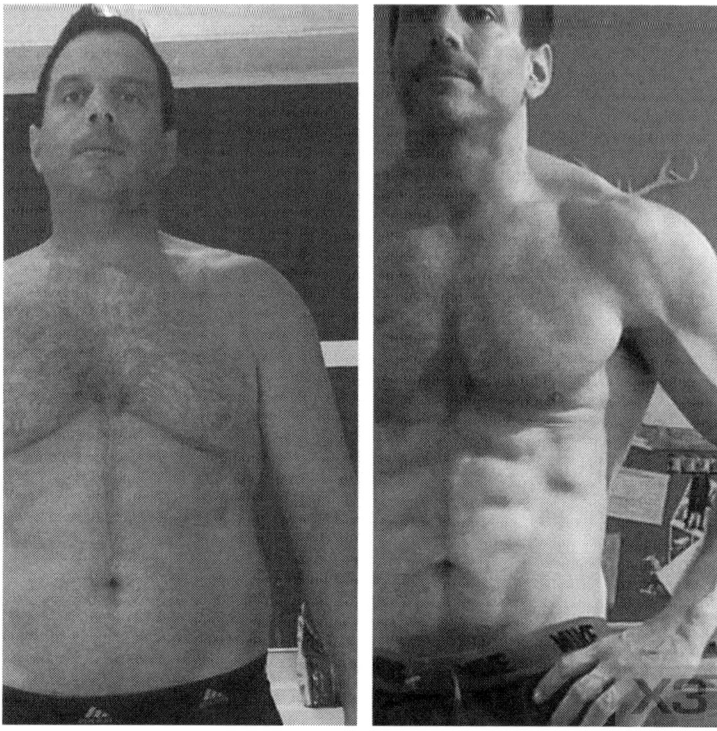

John Ferro's X3 journey started one year ago. "My wife made a joke and said good morning 209, referring to my weight." The comment struck a chord, and Ferro resolved to lose weight and get healthier.

In the first twelve weeks following the X3 programming, Ferro went from being unable to do a pain-free push-up to doing the chest press exercise with the Elite band—which provides about 500 pounds of peak force! In that same time, he started to lose fat and gain muscle. As he looked back on the first twelve weeks, Ferro was stunned by his own progress. "This program is second to none. You get out what you put in. The potential results are unreal."

After just seventeen weeks, Ferro reached his goal weight of 175 pounds. "I spent thirteen years trying everything under the sun to get back in shape from my younger days only to shrink then swell or hurt. This has worked for me in the first seventeen weeks where nothing else has."

Now on week fifty-nine, Ferro is down to 169 pounds and has experienced a truly awe-inspiring transformation. So far he's lost twenty-two pounds of fat and gained eight pounds of muscle. If you're wondering how X3 has affected the jokes from John's wife, he says: "I lifted my shirt and asked my wife if my abs are coming in. She responded sarcastically, 'I hate you.'" Ferro's wife, who has been an avid fitness enthusiast for many years, has recently started training with X3.

MAYKELL LORENZO

Quick Stats: An avid weightlifter, Maykell gained twenty-five pounds of muscle and decreased from 16 percent to 10 percent body fat in ten months after switching to X3 exclusively. Maykell has also become one of the most knowledgeable and helpful X3 users, advising countless other customers on the X3 online forums and meticulously documenting his own progress and workouts.

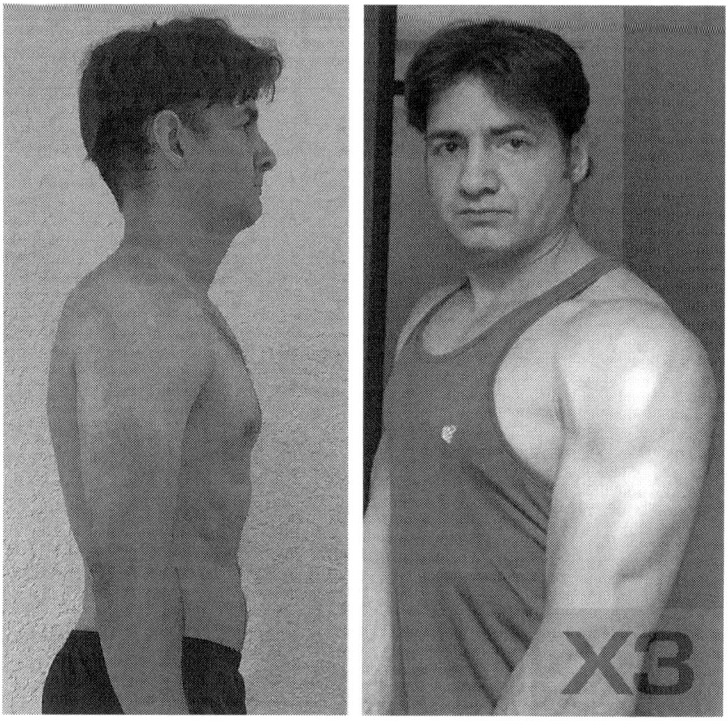

Maykell Lorenzo is a long-time fitness enthusiast and weightlifter who has been consistently training for over fifteen years. In spite of his dedication, he says he's never really gained any size. "I have deadlifted 505 pounds, benched 305 pounds, shoulder pressed 185 pounds (which is more than my body weight), squatted 385 pounds, and I still looked like I needed to eat and like I never worked out."

After the first twelve weeks, Lorenzo was amazed to discover that despite having a very low starting body fat percentage (in the neighborhood of 16 percent) his scale weight dropped about seven pounds, and according to the measurements he was taking, he continued to grow in size. "Okay, now, this is amazing to me. I weighed more twelve weeks ago but look bigger now.

If that is not body recomposition, I don't know what is. I have deadlifted a lot of weight in my life. I'm proud to have done three reps bent-over row at 225 pounds while weighing only 145 pounds at the time, but all of that never made my back grow like this." Lorenzo also claims he has seen better leg growth with X3 than he did in his fifteen years of weightlifting, and his progress pictures support the claim.

Lorenzo keeps a running log of every workout he's ever done with the X3, including which band he used for each exercise and how many reps he managed to get in. He also constantly tracks his changes for overall body weight, body fat percentage, physical measurements in inches, and his caloric intake. In ten months, Lorenzo had worked his way up to 168 pounds—a gain of twenty-five pounds—while at the same time showing a lower body fat percentage than where he started. In his daily update he posts, "Achieved complete and total failure on all moves. It takes a long time to actually learn how that should feel."

Nearly a year and a half after starting his journey, Lorenzo is amazed to see that he is still growing. "I'm always trying to get a better stimulus with each contraction. Slow and controlled reps do make a difference. Since I started implementing them with much more intensity, I feel I'm growing faster now than when I started." To date, he's put on over twenty-five pounds of muscle while maintaining about 10 percent body fat, versus 16 percent body fat when he was weightlifting immediately prior to X3. While he is clearly putting in the work for these kinds of results, Lorenzo in part attributes his success with X3 to his ability to stay consistent. "Remember, consistency pays off. Especially if you are a hard gainer. The ability to safely lift every day without taking weeks off due to injury really makes a difference."

TODD STRATTON

Quick Stats: Todd had success with weightlifting (deadlifting 495 pounds, squatting 450 pounds, and benching 330 pounds), but after suffering from Lyme Disease he was struggling to recover his muscular size despite spending hours in the gym. He switched to X3 and to date has put on twenty-six pounds of muscle while dropping from 10 percent body fat to around 8 percent. Todd also briefly returned to the gym to test his strength and smashed his previous PRs for lifts with regular weights.

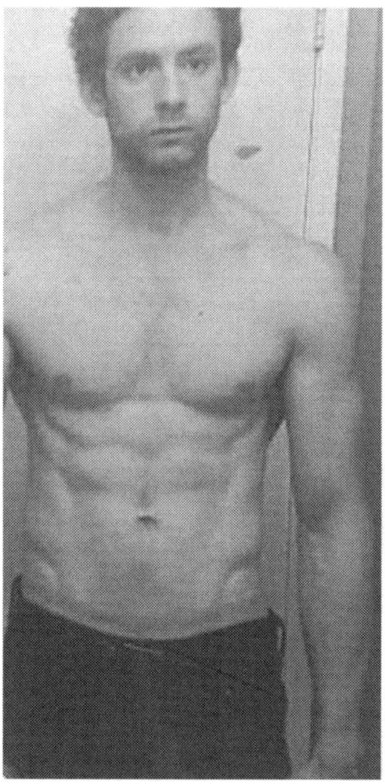

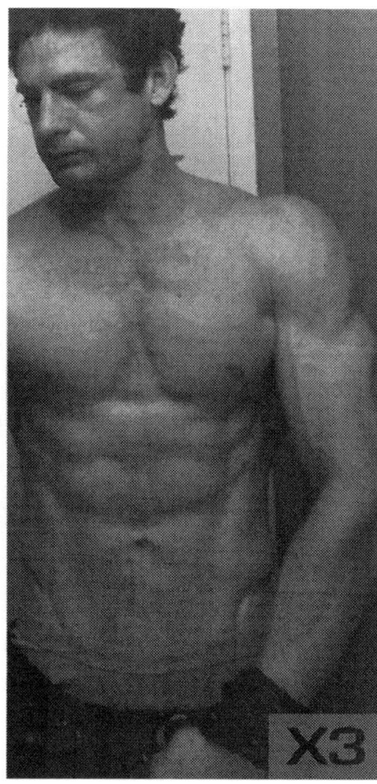

Todd Stratton has been engaged in some form of resistance training since the age of fifteen. In his early twenties, he contracted Lyme Disease, which put a halt to his training for the better part of a year and took a heavy toll on the physique he had worked so hard to achieve. Once he recovered, his goal was merely to get back to where he left off, but since the illness, he says weight gain has been a struggle. Despite spending four to five days a week in the gym, Stratton says, "Sadly my body weight and muscular size have hovered around the same the past three years straight. I put a lot of work into my eating, sleeping well, and workouts each day, so I just want to get to the point where that's obvious."

Being so familiar with resistance training helped Stratton to realize the benefits of the X3 almost immediately. "My muscles are shaking—I have never felt my muscles get hit so deeply before. It just feels way more efficient than regular weight training for me. I can hit the muscles hard, get a lot of stimulation and stress on them without compromising my joints. And I'm also able to get it done much, much faster."

Stratton's previous lifting experience also allowed him to fully embrace the most important aspects of the programming. "Make sure you go to complete and utter failure every set of each exercise. You have to make every set 100 percent effort. It feels like you aren't doing enough because the workouts are so short. But building muscle and getting lean is about stimulation, protein synthesis, and growth hormone." It only took two weeks of working out with the X3 for Stratton to start noticing changes to his physique. "I've never seen myself make these kinds of size gains this quickly before. Especially without taking any kind of supplements."

After a few months of using exclusively the X3, Stratton joined his friends in the gym to test his progress, which turned out to be significant. "I am stronger on every lift I did and came in the gym bigger and leaner. I'm gaining strength and size with just the X3 and the proof is all there with quantifiable and measurable results to show. All my lifts went up by at least ten to twenty pounds."

After five months, Stratton's progress was becoming obvious not only to him, but to the people around him. In that time he had gained fourteen pounds without putting on any real body fat. "People who haven't seen me in a few months started asking how my shoulders and arms grew so much. I told them I haven't lifted regular weights in five months. The look of confusion is priceless. I am having better gains with X3 than I had in the gym no matter what program I was using the past few years."

By the six-month mark, Stratton had grown several inches in his chest and nearly two inches on his arms and calves. Meanwhile, his waist measurement stayed the same, and he was quickly approaching a net gain of twenty pounds. His scale weight was continuing to increase, though his caliper measurements showed an overall drop in body fat from an already very lean physique. Around this time Stratton had a blood panel done and was surprised to discover that his testosterone levels were very low. "I was kind of shocked that my levels were so low, and also surprised I was able to make muscle gains at all and stay lean with testosterone levels that were so low."

Stratton's been committed to the X3 programming for a little over a year and has already exceeded his original strength and physique goals. To date, he has put on twenty-six pounds of muscle while dropping from 10 percent body-fat levels to around 8 percent. "To me preventing injuries while being able to maintain and grow muscle is the biggest selling point. I used to get injured in the gym all the time (random tweaks and aches), and I could never lift as heavy as I needed to grow without stressing my joints at the same time. X3 resolves all those issues."

CHAPTER 6

OPTIMIZING NUTRITION

Through scientific research, we developed X3 to be the optimal fitness tool in terms of increasing strength and decreasing fat. But to be as lean and as strong as possible, you have to do more than just exercise properly. To maximize your results, your nutrition needs to be based on science as well.

ESSENTIAL MACRONUTRIENTS

Nutritionally, there are only two macronutrients: fat and protein. You might be surprised to learn that carbohydrates, although easily converted into energy, are not essential to human life at all. In fact, research has shown that carbohydrates are not needed by any system of the body. As the U.S. Food and Nutrition Board 2005 textbook states, "The lower limit of dietary carbohydrate compatible with life apparently is zero."[70] Contrast that with the Merriam-Webster definition of macronutrient: "a chemical element or substance (such as potassium or protein) that is essential in relatively large amounts to the growth and

70 US Food and Nutrition Board's 2005 textbook. Dietary Reference Intakes for Energy, Carbohydrate, Fiber, Fat, Fatty Acids, Cholesterol, Protein, and Amino Acids. 275-277.

health of a living organism."[71] That's right—as an inessential substance, carbohydrates are by definition not macronutrients for humans. Therefore, it can be concluded that nutrition requirements need only to be considered in the context of consuming the proper amount of proteins and fats.

PROTEIN

Researchers from two other separate studies determined 2.4 grams per kilogram of body weight each day as the optimal level of protein intake. Following this recommendation, if you weigh 200 pounds, this would mean consuming 218 grams of protein daily to maximize your muscle-building potential. However, it is worth noting that this research was done using whey protein, which has been shown to be a less efficient protein source than eggs, meats, and cheeses.[72,73]

John adheres to the 2.2 to 2.5 grams of protein per kilogram of body weight recommendation, a medium to high level compared to the studies cited, and meets his daily needs through a carnivore diet. That might mean eating three pounds of rib eye steak, five to ten eggs and two pounds of ground beef, or several pounds of dark meat chicken each day.

---

71 Merriam-Webster. (n.d.). Macronutrient. In *Merriam-Webster.com dictionary*. Retrieved March 9, 2020, from https://www.merriam-webster.com/dictionary/macronutrient.

72 Antonio, J., Peacock, C. A., Ellerbroek, A., Fromhoff, B., & Silver, T. (2014). The effects of consuming a high protein diet (4.4 g/kg/d) on body composition in resistance-trained individuals. *Journal of the International Society of Sports Nutrition, 11*(1), 19.

73 Longland, T. M., Oikawa, S. Y., Mitchell, C. J., Devries, M. C., & Phillips, S. M. (2016). Higher compared with lower dietary protein during an energy deficit combined with intense exercise promotes greater lean mass gain and fat mass loss: a randomized trial. *The American Journal of Clinical Nutrition, 103*(3), 738-746.

Amino Acids: The Building Blocks of Protein

Amino acids are the building blocks of protein. There are over two hundred in total, some toxic and some essential to human life. An essential amino acid is defined as "one which cannot be synthesized by the animal organism out of materials ordinarily available to the cells at a speed commensurate with the demands for normal growth."[74]

Twenty-one of the existing amino acids are required for protein synthesis in human tissue, including repair and growth of musculature. Of the twenty-one needed, nine cannot be created by the body, including:

- Isoleucine
- Leucine
- Lysine
- Methionine
- Phenylalanine
- Threonine
- Tryptophan
- Valine
- Histidine*

The Histidine Controversy

Technically, histidine is considered an essential amino acid for humans; however, the research supporting the inclusion of histidine as an essential amino acid differs substantially from the research supporting the other eight essential amino acids.

74 Borman, A., T.R. Wood, H.C. Black, E.G. Anderson, M.J. Oesterling, M. Womack and W.C. Rose. (1946). The role of arginine in growth with some observations on the effects of argininic acid. *J. Biol. Chem.* 166: 585.

To be clear, in infancy we must get histidine through our diet, just like any other essential amino acid. But by the time we reach adulthood, our bodies develop significant compensatory mechanisms responding to an absence of dietary histidine. This response is sufficiently effective, as the researchers publishing the original paper identifying essential amino acids for humans concluded, "Histidine is not essential. This surprising result was repeatedly tested; to date, 42 subjects have been kept in N equilibrium on histidine-free diets."[75]

About twenty-five years later in 1975, a longer running study provided evidence that histidine was in fact essential for healthy adults,[76] which is now the most frequent reference for this widely held conclusion.

It may be interesting to note, however, that a 2002 study published in *The Journal of Nutrition* evaluated the long-term effects of histidine deprivation and concluded the following: "The extensive metabolic accommodation, together with decreases in Hb, albumin and transferrin during histidine depletion, leaves unresolved the issue of whether histidine is a dietary essential amino acid in healthy adults."[77] During the course of that study, four individuals consumed a histidine-free diet for forty-eight days without reporting the experience of any side effects, although the absence of histidine did have measurable metabolic impacts. This outcome is different from that seen for the other eight essential amino acids in the original study men-

75 Rose, W. C. (1949). Amino acid, requirements of man. In Federation Proceedings. Federation of American Societies for Experimental Biology (Vol. 8, pp. 546-652).

76 Kopple, J. D., & Swendseid, M. E. (1975). Evidence that histidine is an essential amino acid in normal and chronically uremic man. *The Journal of Clinical Investigation*, 55(5), 881-891.

77 Kriengsinyos, W., Rafii, M., Wykes, L. J., Ball, R. O., & Pencharz, P. B. (2002). Long-term effects of histidine depletion on whole-body protein metabolism in healthy adults. *The Journal of Nutrition*, 132(11), 3340-3348.

tioned earlier, where substantial negative effects were reported after just six days of amino acid deprivation.

Amino Acids and Exercise

When exercising, muscle can only be created if all essential amino acids are available in sufficient quantities for growth. If just one is missing, this anabolic process cannot be completed. If one is in short supply, less lean mass can be created.

Amino acids are utilized by the body through one of two kinds of processes: *anabolism*, which refers to the processes whereby the body builds more complicated molecules out of smaller building blocks, and *catabolism*, meaning the breakdown of complex substances into simpler ones often used to meet energy demands. When amino acids follow the anabolic pathway, they act as building blocks and are synthesized into the proteins that compose muscle itself. As this is their most basic function, the amino acid in the anabolic pathway is fully utilized by the body and no nitrogen or metabolic waste is released from that amino acid.

When amino acids follow the catabolic pathway, they are deaminated—which means an amino group is removed—and the remainder of the molecule is broken down for use as energy. In this process, the amino acid is not used to build protein and the deamination releases nitrogen waste products. We can determine how efficient a protein is at muscle tissue development or repair by comparing the amount of nitrogen-containing catabolic by-products passing through the body in urine and fecal waste with the total amount of nitrogen ingested as protein during that same time period.

Evaluating Protein Sources

The primary driver of protein usability is how well it provides the body with the appropriate amino acids in proportions that match the body's anabolic requirements. When the body is called upon to synthesize protein in muscle, it begins to specifically assimilate the proper amino acids to construct the required tissue. Access to the right amino acids and protein is therefore critical for health.

Not all protein sources are created equal, however. The extent to which proteins are actually utilized by the body depends on the type consumed. In general, the body utilizes eggs best, followed by meat sources, then cheeses, and lastly, whey and vegetable sources, like soy or broccoli.

Research demonstrates the efficiency of each. Egg protein usage approaches the 50 percent mark, while 40 percent of ingested meat protein is used in an anabolic manner. Whey protein, which is quite popular in the athletic industry and is relatively well regarded, has been shown to achieve just 18 percent anabolic usage in human subjects.[78] Vegetable protein sources came in even lower, at under 14 percent.[79] For an athlete trying to promote lean tissue growth through whey protein consumption, this means more than eight out of every ten grams ingested may not be used for its intended purpose.

Supplementing Protein Intake

Most people wish they had more muscle. However, many find

---

78 Lucà-Moretti, M. (1998). A Comparative, Double-blind, Triple Crossover Net Nitrogen Utilization Study Confirms the Discovery of the Master Amino Acid Pattern. Age (years), 152(176), 41-5.

79 Hoffman, J. R., & Falvo, M. J. (2004). Protein–which is best?. *Journal of Sports Science & Medicine, 3*(3), 118.

it hard to meet the recommended daily protein requirement for muscle maximization through diet alone. It may seem inconvenient, expensive, or not compatible with their eating patterns. Although John enjoys eating three or four steaks every day, not everyone feels the same way.

Bodybuilders often use a "bulking and cutting" strategy in an attempt to increase lean mass. In the bulking phase, they eat high levels of protein in a caloric surplus. In the cutting phase, they eat at a caloric deficit in an attempt to reduce body fat without sacrificing the muscle built during the bulking phase. Many find this a frustrating model to follow because of its cyclical nature, adding and then subtracting fat in an attempt to maximize muscle. The scientific nutrition challenge then becomes: how can we create a more efficient protein so that muscle growth can be maximized without requiring a caloric surplus?

It has been proven in multiple studies that a calorie surplus is not what enables muscle growth. Instead, the appropriate level of higher quality protein does. Stated differently, a person can be at a caloric deficit and trigger body fat loss while at the same time growing muscle, given the proper level of protein.[80,81]

In two trials, researchers tested a combination of amino acids designed for the most anabolic effect. These showed lower nitrogen waste than ever measured before. Participants taking the

80 Antonio, J., Peacock, C. A., Ellerbroek, A., Fromhoff, B., & Silver, T. (2014). The effects of consuming a high protein diet (4.4 g/kg/d) on body composition in resistance-trained individuals. *Journal of the International Society of Sports Nutrition, 11*(1), 19.

81 Longland, T. M., Oikawa, S. Y., Mitchell, C. J., Devries, M. C., & Phillips, S. M. (2016). Higher compared with lower dietary protein during an energy deficit combined with intense exercise promotes greater lean mass gain and fat mass loss: a randomized trial. *The American Journal of Clinical Nutrition, 103*(3), 738-746.

superior amino acids showed 33 percent more muscle growth than the control group and had a decline in body fat as well.[82,83]

We leveraged this information to take yet another step forward in the fitness industry. We utilized the best and latest nutritional research to develop the most efficient, effective, low-calorie protein supplement available. Using continuous fermentation chromatography, a process that separates amino acids from fermentation culture, we created a superior amino acid compound like the one used in this study. We then used reverse osmosis to remove water from the culture and, combined with the chromatography process, significantly increase the efficiency of production.

Both meats and plants can ferment. Because our ancestors were not able to refrigerate meats, much of what they ate began to break down before consumption and the resultant by-products of fermentation were routinely ingested. Basically, humans are supposed to eat rotting things, but to avoid infection and other risks, we generally don't. We can now leverage this obvious benefit without the dangers normally associated with food products exposed to air.

We call our latest invention Fortagen, a protein replacement five times more anabolic than standard protein sources. Substituting ten grams (one serving) of Fortagen for fifty grams of ordinary protein creates less work for the digestive system, keeps you at a lower caloric intake, and increases anabolic usage so the max-

---

82 Lucà-Moretti, M. (1998). A Comparative, Double-blind, Triple Crossover Net Nitrogen Utilization Study Confirms the Discovery of the Master Amino Acid Pattern. Age (years), 152(176), 41-5.

83 Pasiakos, S. M., McClung, H. L., McClung, J. P., Margolis, L. M., Andersen, N. E., Cloutier, G. J., ...& Young, A. J. (2011). Leucine-enriched essential amino acid supplementation during moderate steady state exercise enhances post-exercise muscle protein synthesis–. *The American Journal of Clinical Nutrition*, 94(3), 809-818.

imum amount of muscle can be built while getting or staying as lean as possible. With Fortagen, the body uses almost one hundred percent of your protein intake for muscle synthesis, and a single serving has only four calories.

FAT

Fat is the most satiating nutrient. Without enough fat it is much harder, and will require many more calories, to feel full. That's why if you eat only lean chicken breasts, an hour later you're hungry.

In general, steak and eggs already have enough fat in them, so there's no need to add any extra to your diet. Contrary to what many of us have been taught to believe, the healthiest kind of fat may be animal fat—and by this we do mean saturated fat.

Debunking Nutritional Science "Facts"

Saturated fat has gotten a bad reputation in the popular press, and to a lesser extent, in the field of nutrition "science." We've put the word science in quotes because much of what passes as science in the field of nutrition is merely the process of surveying people and then identifying correlations between variables in that data. Many nutrition "scientists" take this a step further by speculating on the existence of causal relationships based on that survey data. Most researchers understand causation can't be determined using this kind of observation, yet that doesn't prevent some of them from reaching for conclusions that all but officially declare a demonstrated cause-and-effect relationship.

As an example, in 2012, the *Archives of Internal Medicine* published a study reviewing data from over 120,000 people participating in the Health Professionals Follow-up Study (1986-2008) and the Nurses' Health Study (1980-2008). The authors divided the study population into five groups, or quintiles, based on their relative consumption of red meat. The first quintile consumed the least red meat, the fifth quintile consumed the most, and the intermediate three quintiles spanned the range of consumption in between.

The authors concluded, "red meat consumption is associated with an increased risk of total, CVD, and cancer mortality." They additionally noted, "We also estimated that 9.3% of deaths in men and 7.6% in women in these cohorts could be prevented at the end of follow-up if all the individuals consumed fewer than 0.5 servings per day (approximately 42 g/d) of red meat."[84]

The latter statement clearly implies the existence of a cause-based relationship. They said, in effect, "IF all individuals consumed fewer than .5 servings per day of red meat, THEN 9.3% of deaths in men and 7.6% of deaths in women would be prevented." They've dodged the use of the word "cause," but the nature of the statement is unambiguous. If, then. Cause and effect.

Mainstream media picked up on the article immediately. Gizmodo's headline *Red Meat Is Responsible for 10% Of Early Deaths* was typical of the response.[85] In this interpretation, red meat is no longer merely correlated with 10 percent of early deaths, it's "responsible" for them.

---

84 Pan, A., Sun, Q., Bernstein, A. M., Schulze, M. B., Manson, J. E., Stampfer, M. J., & ...Hu, F. B. (2012). Red meat consumption and mortality: results from 2 prospective cohort studies. Archives of internal medicine, 172(7), 555-563.

85 https://www.gizmodo.com.au/2012/03/red-meat-is-responsible-for-10-of-early-deaths/.

Given the quotes released from the study, we can hardly blame the journalists for their interpretation. But the defects inherent to all nutritional epidemiology studies—namely an inherent methodological inability to determine causation—are just the tip of the iceberg on this particular piece of research. As we scrutinized the portion of the research addressing unprocessed red meat (we have no interest in defending "processed" meat, which may contain legitimately harmful non-meat ingredients), we found the "total mortality" claim to be highly suspect, and although we won't delve into them specifically in the interest of avoiding redundancy, the cardiovascular and cancer sub-analyses were similarly devoid of merit.

In the study, lifestyle and demographic data was also included: body mass index (BMI), exercise time per week, alcohol consumption, and whether or not participants smoked. As is typical in the results of surveys like this, meat consumption correlated with increased BMI, decreased weekly exercise, increased alcohol consumption, and smoking.

What's more, the raw data actually showed a *decrease* in death rate when moving from the first quintile (lowest level) of red meat consumption to the third quintile. This small change is not statistically significant, so it is more accurate to say there is simply no change in death rate when moving from Q1 to Q3, despite the fact that the participants in Q3 have a (very slightly) higher BMI, exercise less, drink more alcohol, and smoke more. Once the authors adjust for age-related death outcomes, the hazards ratio for Q1 and Q3 are identical.

Knowing higher BMIs, less time exercising, and more time consuming alcohol and smoking are unhealthy, the researchers could have just as easily alleged based on this data that red meat consumption exerts a positive, protective effect against these other negative health influences. While we believe it isn't possible to prove causation from this data, our point is the data in this study tells such a muddled story it would have been easy to make a completely opposing assumption if the researchers harbored a different bias.

Bafflingly, once the authors attempted to adjust for confounding variables beyond age-related outcomes, the reduced death rate in the raw data actually increased to a risk ratio of 1.10 for Q3. This is particularly puzzling because Q3 is already subject to so many negative traits relative to Q1, it would be reasonable to expect the risk would go down rather than up during this adjustment. (And yes, there is actually a way for researchers to provide evidence of successful adjustment for confounding variables after the fact, but this study did not provide it, although our next example study did.)

Let's look at another similar study examining diet and risk factors to see how effective attempts at adjusting for confounding variables tend to be, and how researchers demonstrate the relative efficacy of such adjustments. Reviewing the NIH-AARP Diet and Health Study cohort of more than 500,000 people and analyzing the data by dividing participants into quintiles of red meat consumption as well as lifestyle factors, researchers observed that as meat consumption increased, so too did the incidence of a variety of known health risk factors, such as smoking, lack of exercise, and alcohol consumption.[86]

So far, the same information as in the previous example. But

86 Sinha, R., Cross, A. J., Graubard, B. I., Leitzmann, M. F., & Schatzkin, A. (2009). Meat intake and mortality: a prospective study of over half a million people. Archives of internal medicine, 169(6), 562-571.

this particular study provided an interesting additional piece of data: it showed the hazard ratios of various negative health outcomes for each quintile of meat consumption, and also each corresponding hazard ratio for accidental death (deaths without a medical cause, such as by car accident or violence). As such, changes in risk for accidental death can be presumed to be unrelated to dietary consumption.

For instance, looking specifically at the male population, risk of accidental death increases with red meat consumption. This is generally consistent with the theme that people who eat red meat also tend to engage in other dangerous activities, which pollute the data set. But here's where it gets really interesting: the authors then attempted to adjust for confounding variables to isolate the effect of red meat. Comparing the fifth quintile to the first, the hazards ratio for accidental death was 1.24 (p=.01) before adjustment, but after adjusting for confounding variables, it increased to 1.26 (p=.008).

If researchers from the study had successfully accounted for all confounding variables, the risk ratio of 1.24 before adjustment should have been reduced towards 1.00. Because accidental deaths are not caused by choice of food consumption, they are by logical necessity the by-product of confounding variables. Thus if the impact of confounding variables had been entirely eliminated, there should have been no statistically significant difference found between the Q1 and Q5 risk ratio. But their adjustment actually *increased* the risk ratio (although not statistically significantly), indicating that all the confounding variables had not been properly accounted for. Amusingly, while the researchers included evidence of this failure in the data, they did not discuss it in the body of the article or the abstract.

Statistical errors and failures to fully account for confounding variables aside, let's consider the reported hazard ratios and put them in context. These are ratios indicating the relative risk of a negative event (for the purposes of our analysis, death) when comparing multiple groups of people. Both studies calibrated the first quintile (lowest meat consumption) as 1.0. For each subsequent quintile, the risk ratio for death was compared to the first quintile.

In the first study, the author's final pooled and adjusted hazard ratio for maximal unprocessed red meat consumption was 1.23. In the second study, it was 1.31. You might wonder how these ratios compare to a behavior known to actually cause a negative health outcome: smoking and lung cancer. For an individual smoking more than 1.5 packs of cigarettes a day as compared to a nonsmoker, the hazard ratio for lung cancer is over 108.[87] That's *two orders of magnitude* greater than the risk ratios seen in these major nutritional studies, from which the researchers are trying to contrive evidence of an effect.

You might get the impression we find the above nutrition research worse than useless—and you'd be correct. You might counter that these investigations are worth the money because they provide people with more data from which to draw a conclusion. If the data were presented without bias, this argument might hold some water. But this is very much *not* the case.

Consider the first study, where cholesterol trended downward as red meat consumption increased. This also means that cholesterol trended downward as risk of death increased. Given the

87 Pesch, B., Kendzia, B., Gustavsson, P., Jöckel, K. H., Johnen, G., Pohlabeln, H., & Wichmann, H. E. (2012). Cigarette smoking and lung cancer—relative risk estimates for the major histological types from a pooled analysis of case-control studies. *International Journal of Cancer, 131*(5), 1210-1219.

preceding two trends, the data could also have been arranged such that the risk of death trended downward as a participant's cholesterol increased.

So a researcher eager to draw unsupported casual associations could have easily implied that red meat causes lower cholesterol levels, or lower cholesterol leads to a higher risk of death. But those trends are invisible to the public unless they have access to (and actually read) the entire study. And what are most people exposed to? The summary of the study was published in the popular press, which potentially contains only misleading information and no data at all. Even those who dig a layer deeper and read the abstract (but not the entire study) will still come away misinformed—and it's certainly the case that many scientists and doctors are guilty of reading only a study abstract.

Thus, if we consider to what extent the study promoted a faulty narrative of one specific causal relationship versus providing people with a fair assessment of all of the relevant data, we think you'll agree that the probable real-world educational outcome skews quite far in the negative direction.

A similarly poorly reported study led to the allegation that red meat consumption is correlated to a higher risk of prostate cancer, despite the fact that the relative risk reported for the highest level of red meat consumption has a 95 percent confidence interval that includes 1.0. In other words, forgetting all of the issues with survey science, there was not even a statistically significant correlation between the highest tier of meat consumption and the incidence of the disease in question. Nonetheless, this study has been cited more than 250 times and was featured in, among other things, the recent movie Game Changers as evidence of a causal link.[88]

Opposite Findings and Correlations

To be clear, not all epidemiological outcomes follow the standard dogma about meat, saturated fat, or cholesterol. Research has also shown correlations between higher saturated fat consumption and reduced risk of death from any cause, including specifically strokes, with no association shown on the risk of myocardial infarction. This same research correlated increased carbohydrate consumption with heightened risk of death.[89] Similar results were found in a study on a different population, this time finding a negative correlation between increased saturated fat consumption and the risk of ischemic heart disease of any type.[90]

There are still more findings with regard to cholesterol that are quite inexplicable in light of the prevailing opinions on the subject. Although LDL cholesterol is referred to as "bad cholesterol" and we've been told lower LDL readings are better, a systematic review of other research concluded, "high LDL-C is inversely associated with mortality in most people over 60 years." As those researchers correctly assert, "this finding is inconsistent

---

88 Michaud, D. S., Augustsson, K., Rimm, E. B., Stampfer, M. J., Willett, W. C., & Giovannucci, E. (2001). A prospective study on intake of animal products and risk of prostate cancer. *Cancer Causes & Control, 12*(6), 557-567.

89 Dehghan, M., Mente, A., Zhang, X., Swaminathan, S., Li, W., Mohan, V., & Amma, L. I. (2017). Associations of fats and carbohydrate intake with cardiovascular disease and mortality in 18 countries from five continents (PURE): a prospective cohort study. *The Lancet, 390*(10107), 2050-2062.

90 Praagman, J., Beulens, J. W., Alssema, M., Zock, P. L., Wanders, A. J., Sluijs, I., & Van Der Schouw, Y. T. (2016). The association between dietary saturated fatty acids and ischemic heart disease depends on the type and source of fatty acid in the European Prospective Investigation into Cancer and Nutrition–Netherlands cohort, 2. *The American Journal of Clinical Nutrition, 103*(2), 356-365.

with the cholesterol hypothesis (i.e., that cholesterol, particularly LDL-C, is inherently atherogenic)."[91]

Of course, this kind of data still does not establish anything beyond an association. To maintain the level of critical analysis provided for the preceding studies, we need to point out that to our eye the second saturated fat study mentioned in this section also overstated the significance of its findings. Specifically, it does this by suggesting it has demonstrated that the substitution of vegetable fats or carbohydrates for saturated fat leads to an increase in the incidence of adverse cardiovascular events. That is an issue of cause and effect beyond the scope of this type of study methodology.

The Real Science Behind the Red Meat, Saturated Fat, and Cholesterol

You might be asking yourself by now: what real scientific evidence exists on this subject? What might lend more clarity to this debate? What do we *really* know?

Most of us assume, given the long history of the U.S. and other governments officially advising people to limit fat consumption, there must be a long history of compelling randomized, controlled trials conclusively demonstrating the dangers of fat. Wrong!

A recent meta-analysis concludes there was no evidence from randomized, controlled trials—meaning, an experiment that was actually performed to test a hypothesis—supporting the

91 Ravnskov, U., Diamond, D. M., Hama, R., Hamazaki, T., Hammarskjöld, B., Hynes, N., ...& McCully, K. S. (2016). Lack of an association or an inverse association between low-density-lipoprotein cholesterol and mortality in the elderly: a systematic review. *BMJ open*, *6*(6), e010401.

1977 adoption of national U.S. dietary guidelines suggesting the limitation of fat.[92] Because of the cost, difficulty, and ethical considerations of running RCTs featuring substantial time duration testing of nutritional interventions, there is not as much data to examine as we would like. But what we find from existing analyses is quite interesting.

One randomized, controlled trial performed with participants from mental hospitals and a nursing home compared a standard diet, including a more substantial portion of saturated-fat intake, with a test diet substituting vegetable fats for much of the saturated fats. Conducted from 1968 until 1973, when ethical standards were more lax, it is unlikely that such a study will be attempted anytime soon. While the study was meant to demonstrate how a low animal fat diet could be used to reduce serum cholesterol (LDL-C) and thereby reduce the incidence of cardiovascular events, the data did not support that conclusion, so it was largely suppressed at the time.[93] Fortunately, the data were recently rediscovered, and a more complete review of those data was published by The BMJ (this journal was once called the *British Medical Journal* but now is titled by the acronym alone, much like KFC) in 2016. What the data actually showed was that while substituting vegetable oils for animal fats lowered cholesterol, it had no effect in terms of reducing cardiovascular (or other) deaths. If anything, higher cholesterol levels correlated with reduced risk of death! Hardly the popular narrative.

---

92 Harcombe, Z., Baker, J. S., Cooper, S. M., Davies, B., Sculthorpe, N., DiNicolantonio, J. J., & Grace, F. (2015). Evidence from randomized, controlled trials did not support the introduction of dietary fat guidelines in 1977 and 1983: a systematic review and meta-analysis. *Open Heart*, 2(1), e000196.

93 Ramsden, C. E., Zamora, D., Majchrzak-Hong, S., Faurot, K. R., Broste, S. K., Frantz, R. P., ...& Hibbeln, J. R. (2016). Re-evaluation of the traditional diet-heart hypothesis: analysis of recovered data from Minnesota Coronary Experiment (1968-73). *BMJ*, *353*, i1246.

Other more-modern, randomized, controlled trials on high-fat diets show generally positive outcome trends. A small study on ketogenic diets showed increased HDL with stable LDL, considered indicative of a lowered risk of a bad cardiac event.[94] Likewise, study participants with the possibly pathological Type B LDL condition (smaller average LDL particles) saw a significant increase in LDL particle size—generally seen as favorable because smaller LDL particles are likely more inflammatory than larger particles and may be associated with atherosclerosis. The high-fat diet substantially lowered blood triglyceride levels to under that of people eating lower fat meals. Again, this represents an improvement in terms of reducing traditional cardiovascular risk factors. Another longer study with more participants revealed high-fat ketogenic diets trumping low-fat diets for HDL cholesterol improvement and lowering (very ironically) triglycerides with no statistical difference in LDL.[95]

Lest you think the only benefit shown above was due to the diet being a specific doctor-monitored ketogenic diet, an additional randomized, controlled trial conducted by Stanford researchers compared the extremely low-carb, high-fat, high-protein Atkins Diet to other more conventional diet protocols and concluded those who were assigned to "the Atkins diet, which had the lowest carbohydrate intake, lost more weight and experienced more favorable overall metabolic effects at 12

94 Sharman, M. J., Kraemer, W. J., Love, D. M., Avery, N. G., Gómez, A. L., Scheett, T. P., & Volek, J. S. (2002). A ketogenic diet favorably affects serum biomarkers for cardiovascular disease in normal-weight men. *The Journal of Nutrition, 132*(7), 1879-1885.

95 Yancy, W. S., Olsen, M. K., Guyton, J. R., Bakst, R. P., & Westman, E. C. (2004). A low-carbohydrate, ketogenic diet versus a low-fat diet to treat obesity and hyperlipidemia: a randomized, controlled trial. *Annals of Internal Medicine, 140*(10), 769-777.

months than women assigned to follow the Zone, Ornish, or LEARN diets."[96]

If we focus on research that includes actual experimentation—in other words, real science rather than survey taking—the popular view of ideal nutrition appears generally unfounded. On the subject of cholesterol, some if not THE only randomized, controlled trials supporting the "bad cholesterol" hypothesis were done using statins (or similar pharmaceuticals) to lower LDL in a test group and then evaluating outcomes over time. Many actually showed a survival benefit, but this might just demonstrate that the drugs involved have some cardioprotective effect other than merely lowering LDL-C. As evidence of this possibility, consider that a 12,000-person randomized, controlled trial on a different pharmaceutical (evacetrapib) found a "31.1% decrease in the mean LDL cholesterol level was observed with evacetrapib versus a 6.0% increase with placebo," but was terminated early at the twenty-six-week mark due to lack of efficacy because "evacetrapib did not result in a lower rate of cardiovascular events than placebo." At the termination of the experiment, the cardiovascular event rate was 12.8 percent in the placebo group, and 12.9 percent in the evacetrapib group despite the greatly lowered LDL-C numbers in the latter group.

Your LDLs go up if you fast for forty-eight hours because your body is metabolizing its own body fat. Simply saying that high levels of LDLs are bad for you is like saying fat loss is bad for you. People who are losing body fat are less likely to have a heart attack, not more likely to have one.

96 Gardner, C. D., Kiazand, A., Alhassan, S., Kim, S., Stafford, R. S., Balise, R. R., ...& King, A. C. (2007). Comparison of the Atkins, Zone, Ornish, and LEARN diets for change in weight and related risk factors among overweight premenopausal women: the A TO Z Weight Loss Study: a randomized trial. *Jama*, 297(9), 969-977.

X3 NUTRITION OPTIMIZATION

Through our research, we've developed some practical advice to optimize your nutrition. Whether you want to lose weight, build muscle, or simply be as healthy as possible, these recommendations still apply. You may choose to implement one or all of these suggestions, depending on how serious you are about achieving your goals.

ELIMINATE SUGAR

The first thing we recommend is to cut out added sugar. Dietary sugar is the leading factor in obesity. In general, you don't get fat from eating fat, you get fat from eating too much sugar as well as other kinds of carbohydrates. People often get angry when we tell them to cut crackers, cookies, and candy from their diet. It's like trying to take a drug away from an addict.

There's a reason why processed food companies love to put sugar in their products. It keeps you hungry and coming back for more. That's how you can have an entire bowl of chips in front of you one minute, then all of a sudden, you reach down and realize the entire bag is gone.

The downsides of sugar are broadly understood and not controversial, so we won't spend time diving into the research. If you want to better understand this issue, we recommend that you start by searching for content from Professor Robert H. Lustig.

ELIMINATE SIMPLE CARBOHYDRATES

As we stated earlier in this chapter, carbohydrates are not a macronutrient. They are not required by the body to function, nor do they help it function more efficiently. Like sugar, carbohydrates keep you hungry all the time. So, our second recommendation is to cut out processed carbohydrates. This includes eliminating processed grains, like anything made from flour, from your diet.

The sole differentiator of carbohydrates in human nutrition is the ease with which they put on body fat. As an evolutionary response, this lines up with when things are available in nature. For instance, a bear comes out of hibernation and eats protein—say deer and a fish—until the end of the summer. In autumn, when carbohydrates become available again, they eat as many fruits and berries as possible. Bears basically give themselves type two diabetes every year before they go into hibernation in an attempt to get as fat as possible. With that much adipose tissue, the bear can better manage cold temperatures, live off its body fat, and go months without eating.

The bottom line: if you're looking to increase your body fat, eat carbohydrates. If you're looking for optimal health, focus on fats and proteins.

DO INTERMITTENT FASTING/TIME-RESTRICTED EATING

Research shows fasting is one of the healthiest things you can do for your body. It provides a total metabolic reset, autophagy, and regeneration of the immune system. Fasting effectively gives the body time to repair itself. There are also major hormonal benefits that come along with time-restricted eating; when you fast for a certain amount of time a day, your body produces more growth hormone.[97]

97 Ho, K. Y., Veldhuis, J. D., Johnson, M. L., Furlanetto, R., Evans, W. S., Alberti, K. G., & Thorner, M. O. (1988). Fasting enhances growth hormone secretion and amplifies the complex rhythms of growth hormone secretion in man. *The Journal of Clinical Investigation*, *81*(4), 968-975.

For most of human history, we didn't eat three square meals a day because we didn't have food available at all times. If people were going without food because they hadn't killed an animal recently, the body burned fat to get necessary nutrients and have enough energy to survive. Looking through this type of evolutionary lens, eating breakfast, lunch, and dinner every day is unnatural.

Interestingly, fasting has been recognized as an effective health intervention for thousands of years. It may well be the case that early humans recognized the benefits of fasting almost as soon as they developed agriculture and thereby the ability to engage in unhealthier habits of continuous food consumption. In the context of more recent history, Mark Twain once wrote, "A little starvation can really do more for the average sick man than can the best medicines and the best doctors. I do not mean a restricted diet; I mean total abstention from food for one or two days."[98] That observation turns out to be quite prescient and now we have the scientific evidence to back it up.

Isn't Fasting Just a Way to Achieve Caloric Restriction?

Fortunately, fasting and time-restricted feeding are not merely a caloric restriction. This is good because caloric restriction doesn't work particularly well, and that's why so few people have success losing (and keeping off) weight with calorie-restricted diets. If this is surprising, consider the Women's Health Initiative, the most ambitious, important weight-loss study ever undertaken. This enormous, randomized trial involving almost 50,000 women evaluated a low-fat, low-calorie approach to weight loss. Through intensive counseling, women were per-

98 Twain, M. (1899). My debut as a literary person. Century Company.

suaded to reduce their daily caloric intake by 342 calories and increase exercise by 10 percent. Researchers projected a weight loss of thirty-two pounds over a SINGLE year based on their understanding of thermodynamics.

When the final results were tallied in 2006, the experiment proved the opposite of conventional thinking. Despite good compliance, over seven years of calorie counting led to virtually no weight loss (.04kg). Not even a single pound.[99] Therefore, something—that we now know is the endocrine system—must have superseded the overly simplified thermodynamic arithmetic associated with the concept of caloric restriction.

Of course, while the above results reflect extremely poorly on the efficacy of caloric restriction as a dietary intervention meant to promote weight loss, they don't show that intermittent fasting offers any advantage. And they don't thoroughly debunk the allegation that the total number of calories consumed over a given time period is the only mechanism by which diets exert any effect on body weight. That last argument may seem strange, but we are presented with it quite often, and its proponents tend to suggest that it is a "law of physics," which of course oversimplifies the chemical energy pathways of the body to the point of inaccuracy.

Fortunately, you don't have to take our word on this, as a recent randomized, controlled trial demonstrated quite conclusively that when it comes to time-restricted eating, there are benefits for obesity and health generally that are not derived from caloric restriction. This study took mice and fed them a high-fat diet. This diet was designed to be unhealthy, as it typically leads

---

99 Howard, et al. (2006). Low-fat dietary pattern and weight change over 7 years: the Women's Health Initiative Dietary Modification Trial. *JAMA*. Jan 4;295(1):39-49.

to insulin resistance, Type 2 Diabetes, and fatty liver disease in mice. Researchers then divided the mice into multiple different groups. One had food available twenty-four hours a day, while the other was only permitted to eat within an eight-hour window. Both of those groups consumed the same food and the same amount of calories.

At the end of the experiment, the group of mice that was able to eat whenever they wanted developed all the usual pathologies associated with this kind of diet. The time-restricted eating group, however, did not become obese, develop insulin-resistance problems, or have fatty liver disorder. Simply by restricting the time within which mice ate their meals, the negative health consequences normally associated with the high-fat diet were eliminated. The researchers concluded that a "time-restricted feeding regimen is a non-pharmacological strategy against obesity and associated diseases."[100]

Just to reiterate, mice in both groups consumed the same number of calories every day, and the same type of food, but the time-restricted eating mice lived longer, were not obese, and were healthier according to every measure the researchers considered. This effectively falsifies the hypothesis that diet outcomes such as weight loss stem only from changing the number of calories consumed, since both groups of mice consumed the same number of calories. Additionally, and perhaps more surprisingly, this also proves that when you eat could be as important as what you eat.

Now, animal studies are often criticized, but animals don't lie

100 Hatori, M, Vollmers, C, Zarrinpar A, DiTacchio L, Bushong EA, Gill S, Chaix A, Joens M, Fitzpatrick JAJ, Elisman MH, & Panda S. (2012). Time-restricted feeding without reducing caloric intake prevents metabolic diseases in mice fed a high-fat diet. *Cell Metabolism*. 15(6), 848-860.

about how much they ate, how much alcohol they drank, or how many cigarettes they smoked on their surveys. So when we're trying to evaluate a claim about whether or not the diets are more complicated than just modulating calorie intake, animal models are a great way to test, since you really do know what those mice ate and how much of it. Furthermore, when there is both human and animal data, the relevance increases just from a confirmation of evidence perspective.

What Exactly Happens When You Fast?

The body experiences a variety of different physiological changes as you fast, depending on how long you have been fasting. We will go over the research on this fasting timeline now, and then in the next several sections, we will explain some typical approaches to fasting. In effect, we will cover the theory and research, and then provide a brief discussion of how you might implement this.

First, the benefits of fasting appear to occur because after a sufficient period of time without food, a "metabolic switch" is flicked in the body. This typically occurs around twelve hours after your last meal, assuming you consume no further calories during that time.[101] In other words, in the context of health benefits, "fasting" starts after twelve hours without food. Of course, as with all biological quantities, this number varies somewhat from person to person, but on average, this is the correct time window, and if it's only been eight hours since your last meal, you are almost certainly not "fasting" in the way we are using the word.

101 Anton, S. D., Moehl, K., Donahoo, W. T., Marosi, K., Lee, S. A., Mainous III, A. G., ...& Mattson, M. P. (2018). Flipping the metabolic switch: understanding and applying the health benefits of fasting. *Obesity*, 26(2), 254-268.

Around twelve hours after your last consumption of food, the body begins to break fatty acids down into ketone bodies, which will become the new blood-borne chemical energy vector, replacing the glucose that your body is running out of. [102] While we would expect this metabolic switch to be "flipped" at the twelve-hour mark and the transition to ketosis to be initiated at that time, it may take a much longer fast of perhaps seventy-two hours for some individuals to transition completely to a ketogenic state.[103] The amount of time required for that effect is highly dependent on dietary history and fortunately, the benefits of fasting are not dependent on anyone achieving full ketosis. In fact, within twenty-four hours, the body will begin the process of autophagy, wherein it recycles and replaces old cells and cellular components. This process includes the destruction of misfolded proteins, the presence of which has been linked to Alzheimer's and other diseases.[104]

Then, by the forty-eight-hour mark, growth hormone levels peak, on average increasing to five times one's baseline levels.[105] At fifty hours, serum insulin, which has been trending downward since the onset of fasting, typically reaches its minimum

---

102 Mattson MP, Longo VD, Harvie M. Impact of intermittent fasting on health and disease processes. *Ageing Res Rev* 2017;39:46-58.

103 Scott, J. M., & Deuster, P. A. (2017). Ketones and Human Performance. Journal of special operations medicine: a peer reviewed journal for SOF medical professionals, 17(2), 112-116.

104 Alirezaei, M., Kemball, C. C., Flynn, C. T., Wood, M. R., Whitton, J. L., & Kiosses, W. B. (2010). Short-term fasting induces profound neuronal autophagy. *Autophagy, 6*(6), 702-710.

105 Hartman, M. L., Veldhuis, J. D., Johnson, M. L., Lee, M. M., Alberti, K. G., Samojlik, E., & Thorner, M. O. (1992). Augmented growth hormone (GH) secretory burst frequency and amplitude mediate enhanced GH secretion during a two-day fast in normal men. *The Journal of Clinical Endocrinology & Metabolism, 74*(4), 757-765.

level.[106] Keep that insulin statistic in mind when we get to the next section on fasting and testosterone.

Finally, by the seventy-two-hour mark, the body has been triggered to recycle and replace all of its T-Cells, effectively regenerating a substantial part of the immune system and reversing immunosuppression.[107] This last result is profound and only recently discovered. It has the potential to strengthen the immune system and to protect its cells against chemotoxicity, which could come in very handy for the treatment of cancer.

Fasting Has a Surprising Effect on Testosterone

Some of the fasting research discussed above has received significant attention in the health and wellness world and some of our claims there may be familiar. However, there is also a substantial body of research discussing the effect of fasting on testosterone, and we believe this information is much less publicized. This may be surprising because many people think about testosterone and diet in the context of asking what foods can be eaten to increase testosterone levels. This is the opposite of an effective approach. In reality, insulin slows testosterone production in the body, and generally food consumption is associated with insulin release. This discovery is the basis of the relationship between time-restricted eating/fasting and testosterone.

As we just discussed, when we go without food, our bodies undergo changes to utilize the energy from our own body fat

---

106 Klein, S., Sakurai, Y. O. I. C. H. I., Romijn, J. A., & Carroll, R. M. (1993). Progressive alterations in lipid and glucose metabolism during short-term fasting in young adult men. *American Journal of Physiology-Endocrinology and Metabolism*, 265(5), E801-E806.

107 Cheng, C. W., Adams, G. B., Perin, L., Wei, M., Zhou, X., Lam, B. S., ...& Kopchick, J. J. (2014). Prolonged fasting reduces IGF-1/PKA to promote hematopoietic-stem-cell-based regeneration and reverse immunosuppression. *Cell Stem Cell*, *14*(6), 810-823.

and many hormones become triggered to facilitate this process. Testosterone, a primarily male sex hormone, is responsible for the major male-associated characteristics, such as muscle growth, facial hair, bone mass density, and sexual drive. It is also upregulated during the fasting period.

Researchers Habito and Ball demonstrated that the ingestion of both vegetarian and animal-based meals acutely lowered circulating testosterone, except when the meal was composed primarily of fat.[108] This result is consistent with our hypothesis set forth above regarding insulin as a critical factor involved in downregulating testosterone, since fat intake does not promote an insulin response. There have also been several studies that have linked time-restricted eating/fasting to increases in circulating testosterone. Intermittent fasting has been shown to improve the production of luteinizing hormone (LH). In men, this hormone stimulates Leydig cells' production of testosterone.

In one such study, intermittent fasting in healthy men looking to improve testosterone showed an improvement in fasting LH of nearly 67 percent which in turn improved overall testosterone by an amazing 180 percent.[109] Other fasting research shows that this kind of temporary abstention from eating can dramatically assist in improving insulin sensitivity, which naturally promotes increases in testosterone by reducing the amount of insulin the body needs to release.[110] The benefit is also realized because improved insulin sensitivity is associated with the rapid metab-

108 Habito, R. C., & Ball, M. J. (2001). Postprandial changes in sex hormones after meals of different composition. *Metabolism-Clinical and Experimental, 50*(5), 505-511.

109 Röjdmark, S., Asplund, A., & Rössner, S. (1989). Pituitary-testicular axis in obese men during short-term fasting. *European Journal of Endocrinology, 121*(5), 727-732.

110 Sutton, E. F., Beyl, R., Early, K. S., Cefalu, W. T., Ravussin, E., & Peterson, C. M. (2018). Early time-restricted feeding improves insulin sensitivity, blood pressure, and oxidative stress even without weight loss in men with prediabetes. *Cell Metabolism, 27*(6), 1212-1221.

olization of body fat, and lower levels of body fat are associated with higher levels of testosterone.

As we discussed earlier in this chapter, many nutrition "experts" have been saying for years that fasting is just the same as calorie restriction with different meal timing, and therefore should be ignored. We've already thoroughly discredited this claim in other contexts, but let's evaluate how it applies (or doesn't) to testosterone. Given our insulin response hypothesis, you probably already know the answer. We see in the above research that testosterone goes up in periods of fasting.

You might wonder what results are seen in research with regards to testosterone levels when people instead choose to create a caloric deficit while continuing to eat frequently? Strauss and researchers measured testosterone levels in wrestlers during the competitive season, a period when athletes notoriously restrict calories to stay in lower weight classes, and two months post-season. As we would expect, testosterone was lower during the season, and the lowest testosterone was associated with the greatest weight loss. With ordinary caloric restriction, unlike fasting, the reduced calories led to reduced testosterone. Or as the researchers concluded, "These findings suggest that the dietary restriction practiced by some wrestlers may affect serum testosterone levels adversely."[111]

Similarly, a 2010 study concluded, "Serum total testosterone and the free androgen index were significantly lower in the caloric restriction group." This study examined the effect of a low-calorie diet (330 calories/day) on testosterone levels in

111 Strauss, R.H., R.R. Lanese, and W.B. Malarkey. (1985). Weight loss in amateur wrestlers and its effect on serum testosterone levels. *JAMA*. 20;254:3337-8.

overweight women, and after the two-week mark, a 40 percent decrease in free testosterone levels was observed.[112]

So, in the context of the bigger picture, why would time-restricted eating/fasting increase testosterone, whereas caloric restriction would decrease it? We do not yet know enough to definitively describe the mechanisms. However, various researchers have offered a few theories.

One is that your body is always trying to find homeostasis. This means a position of neutrality where all of the systems of the body are in balance and are functioning. Now, if you put the body in a situation where it has zero calories, is it going to find homeostasis for this position? Of course not. This is not sustainable. Instead of trying to adapt to an impossible circumstance, the body instead prepares for the future. It knows you will need to eat something eventually, and to get to that point—say, to potentially catch an animal for consumption—it will help you. This is done by dramatically increasing growth hormone, even upwards of 2,000 percent, to maintain muscle mass all while body fat is being metabolized for energy.[113] Consistent with this goal, circulating testosterone is also increased so that when protein sources are consumed, the process of muscle protein synthesis can begin.

In contrast to this, a low-calorie environment does initiate a homeostasis process, since reduced but continuous calorie

112 Kiddy, D.S. D. Hamilton-Failey, M. Seppala, R. Koistinen, V.H. James, M.J. Reed, and S. Franks. (1989) Diet-induced changes in sex hormone binding globulin and free testosterone in women with normal or polycystic ovaries: correlation with serum insulin and insulin-like growth factor-I. *Clin Endocrinol* (Oxf). 31:757-63.

113 Ho, K. Y., Veldhuis, J. D., Johnson, M. L., Furlanetto, R., Evans, W. S., Alberti, K. G., & Thorner, M. O. (1988). Fasting enhances growth hormone secretion and amplifies the complex rhythms of growth hormone secretion in man. *The Journal of Clinical Investigation*, *81*(4), 968-975.

intake is potentially tenable for the body in a survival context. This means that by regularly eating smaller meals and remaining in a caloric deficit, you potentially send a signal to the body telling it this will be what is consumed moving forward and your body responds to that signal. It's a survival mechanism, so the body can adjust to periods of poor food availability. Instead of triggering growth hormone and testosterone like a zero-calorie period would, cortisol becomes upregulated, so you can keep as much body fat as possible and reduce the amount of muscle you have.[114,115] This is the body's way of adjusting to a lower calorie situation than would normally be required to maintain your current body mass. This is the opposite of what we all want. Therefore, the science leads us to recommend fasting over caloric restriction for everyone.

Yes, we are aware that most bodybuilders have used caloric restriction since the beginning of the "sport," but just because people have been doing something for a long time does not mean they are correct. Those same bodybuilders also perpetually complain about the muscle mass they lose during their contest preparation. Focusing on time-restricted eating/fasting instead can produce more rapid fat loss and induce the preservation of all muscle mass.

It would be fair at this point to object and point out that our evidence so far has been focused on hormonal responses specifically, showing that growth hormone and testosterone are upregulated by fasting. But can we really have confidence that

---

114 Peeters, G. M. E. E., Van Schoor, N. M., Van Rossum, E. F. C., Visser, M., & Lips, P. T. A. M. (2008). The relationship between cortisol, muscle mass and muscle strength in older persons and the role of genetic variations in the glucocorticoid receptor. *Clinical Endocrinology*, 69(4), 673-682.

115 Moyer, A. E., Rodin, J., Grilo, C. M., Cummings, N., Larson, L. M., & Rebuffé-Scrive, M. (1994). Stress-induced cortisol response and fat distribution in women. *Obesity Research*, 2(3), 255-262.

muscle mass is maintained during fasted periods? In fact, we do. Multiple studies have demonstrated that fasting can be undertaken while preserving muscle and losing fat and that fasting can lead to muscle growth after the fasting period.

A 2010 study examined alternate daily fasting and found that fasting subjects were able to lose significant fat mass with no change in lean mass.[116] In that fasting schedule, subjects alternate between days of normal eating and days of fasting. This study also observed numerous metabolic benefits, such as reduced cholesterol, triglycerides, and waist circumference. Similarly, research on daily sixteen-hour fasts performed in 2016 showed that participants in those fasts were also able to lose significant amounts of weight with no loss in muscle mass or maximal strength.[117]

Fasting Triggers an Anabolic Acceleration When It Ends

An intriguing 2016 study compared alternate day fasting with daily calorie restriction among obese subjects who were not engaged in exercise. The subjects engaged in eight weeks of intervention, followed by twenty-four weeks of unmodified follow-up. Measurements were made at the eight-week and thirty-two-week mark. At eight weeks, the fasting group had lost more weight as a percentage of starting weight (marginal significance, p=.056) with otherwise negligible differences between groups. However, at the thirty-two-week follow-up,

---

116 Bhutani, S., Klempel, M. C., Berger, R. A., & Varady, K. A. (2010). Improvements in coronary heart disease risk indicators by alternate-day fasting involve adipose tissue modulations. *Obesity, 18*(11), 2152-2159.

117 Moro, T., Tinsley, G., Bianco, A., Marcolin, G., Pacelli, Q. F., Battaglia, G., ...& Paoli, A. (2016). Effects of eight weeks of time-restricted feeding (16/8) on basal metabolism, maximal strength, body composition, inflammation, and cardiovascular risk factors in resistance-trained males. *Journal of Translational Medicine*, 14(1), 290.

the fasting group had accomplished a statistically significant gain in percent lean muscle mass compared to baseline while the caloric restriction group had not. Also, at thirty-two weeks the fasting group retained a statistically significant decrease in percent body fat, while the caloric restriction group had no such improvement compared to baseline when measured at thirty-two weeks.[118]

We believe that because of the hormonal impacts of fasting, there may have been some lingering effect leading to its superiority over a longer time span. Effectively, it may have "primed" the body to build muscle and not to store fat so when participants presumably abandoned the diet after the eight-week mark, more of their increased caloric intake was diverted to lean mass growth, resulting in the improvement seen at the thirty-two-week mark. Meanwhile, those in the caloric restriction group had no such hormonal benefit and promptly regained the fat that had been lost during the first eight weeks of the study when they were restricted in caloric intake.

It's also interesting to note that in this study, the fasting group lost lean mass during the eight weeks of fasting, but the gains from weeks eight through thirty-two were so significant they overcame the initial loss to produce a statistically significant increase over the baseline values. If you are concerned about the initial loss of lean mass, keep in mind that fasting is not magic and a diet that is too low in calories or protein (and protein especially is easy to under consume) for a prolonged period of time will not be saved by fasting. But as we saw in this study, once caloric intake increased, the fasting participants

118 Catenacci, V. A., Pan, Z., Ostendorf, D., Brannon, S., Gozansky, W. S., Mattson, M. P., ...& Troy Donahoo, W. (2016). A randomized pilot study comparing zero-calorie alternate-day fasting to daily caloric restriction in adults with obesity. *Obesity*, *24*(9), 1874-1883.

were prepared for substantial muscle growth. This is doubly interesting because there is no evidence that any of the participants engaged in exercise of any kind, yet they still grew.

All of this begs a question: is there an anabolic acceleration mechanism at the end of a fast—other than in this study—that is not fully documented yet? We have seen in ourselves that after ending a longer fasted period there seems to be an anabolic acceleration effect lasting a few days where the added muscle mass seems far beyond what one would expect in that amount of time.

When it comes to fasting studies, the one kind of seemingly conflicting research you should look out for involves an unintentionally misleading definition of "fasting." For example, one such study compared a group restricting calories with another group described as a "fasted" group. The problem with this paper is that the "fasted" group consumed 500 calories per day during the "fasting day." So there was no fasting at all in the research—just a calorie-restriction group and a second calorie-restriction group being compared to the first.[119] This, of course, is not actually relevant to the benefits of fasting, since neither group truly fasted, and, as you might expect, it fails to show the benefits usually seen with actual fasting.

Now that we've reviewed the evidence supporting fasting, let's move on to a discussion of how exactly you can implement it, and how we suggest you get started.

119 Trepanowski, J. F., Kroeger, C. M., Barnosky, A., Klempel, M. C., Bhutani, S., Hoddy, K. K., ...& Ravussin, E. (2017). Effect of alternate-day fasting on weight loss, weight maintenance, and cardioprotection among metabolically healthy obese adults: a randomized clinical trial. *JAMA Internal Medicine, 177*(7), 930-938.

16:8 Split

The most basic way to implement intermittent fasting is to do a 16:8 split. This means eating within an eight-hour window and fasting for the remaining sixteen hours. In most cases, people choose to skip breakfast in this method.

Contrary to popular "wisdom," there is no scientific study that shows breakfast is the most important meal of the day. A cereal company came up with that. Breakfast actually slows you down. Anytime you're digesting food, your cognitive function is diminished. You should not be eating when you're about to engage in strenuous mental or physical activity. In fact, we recommend exercising fasted to elicit the most efficient muscular and hormonal response.

Moderate-length fasting like a 16:8 split triggers a hormonal response that prevents you from losing muscle or other valuable tissue while encouraging your body to switch over to burning the tissue that serves the specific function of energy storage. As we mentioned above, fasting begins to exert positive effects after approximately twelve hours in humans, so with 16:8 fasting, the participant enters the fasted state after hour twelve and then spends four hours benefiting from that state before ending the fast. This introductory level recommendation is the threshold where you should start to see benefits from intermittent fasting.

Eat One Meal a Day (OMAD)

The next obvious step in intermittent fasting is to move to one meal a day. That's a 23:1 split, and the concept is simple. You just have dinner or a late lunch every day.

John, for example, regularly consumes two large steaks or two pounds of steak and a rack of ribs for his one meal a day. Your goal is to eat enough and get the proper amount of protein in this single daily meal. Keep in mind, you can follow any sort of diet—for instance, ketogenic, carnivore, or others—while adhering to an OMAD eating pattern. There is no evidence the benefits of fasting are limited to any particular nutrition plan.

Occasionally Fast for Forty-Eight or Seventy-Two Hours

Occasionally fasting for forty-eight or seventy-two hours is a great way to keep your immune system strong. This is something you can do in the context of a more regular eating pattern. This recommendation is not intended for indefinite use, but to be implemented perhaps once a month.

Research done at USC in 2014 shows a seventy-two-hour fast triggers stem cell regeneration of T-Cells.[120] In other words, the entire immune system basically resets after not eating for three days. White blood cells are fully replaced and old ones are sacrificed for fuel by the body.

Bulletproof Coffee and Time-Restricted Eating/Fasting

There's some evidence that consuming less than fifty calories of something during the fasting period does not impact the benefits of time-restricted eating. We also speculate that a lot of the benefit of fasting has to do with the lack of insulin response, so it may even be possible to consume more than fifty calories if all of those calories are from fat, as they would be in the case of Bulletproof Coffee.

---

120 Cheng, C. W., Adams, G. B., Perin, L., Wei, M., Zhou, X., Lam, B. S., ...& Kopchick, J. J. (2014). Prolonged fasting reduces IGF-1/PKA to promote hematopoietic-stem-cell-based regeneration and reverse immunosuppression. *Cell Stem Cell, 14*(6), 810-823.

If we're correct, putting butter or MCT oil in your coffee—popularly known as Bulletproof Coffee—might allow you to maintain your fast while satiating hunger before your first meal of the day. Some people also believe that the presence of fat reduces the rate of absorption of the caffeine, leading to a longer period of benefit with less of a "jittery" feeling. Both John and Henry drank Bulletproof coffee for a short time when first adjusting to fasting but no longer rely on this technique.

IMPLEMENT A KETOGENIC DIET

The next step would be to eliminate many unprocessed carbohydrates as well, including most fruit and starchy vegetables, as well as remaining grains, from your diet. When the quantity of carbohydrates you consume is low enough, this is referred to as a ketogenic diet.

Ketosis refers to a state where the body has created a relatively large quantity of ketone bodies for use as energy transporters in the blood. Ketones are created from fats, and this state is a natural metabolic reaction to an absence of sufficient glucose for the body to meet its energy needs. Effectively, in ketosis, the body uses broken down fat as the standard energy delivery mechanism in the bloodstream instead of glucose. The Standard American Diet (SAD) keeps most people running on glucose, which is transported into the cells with the help of insulin, at all times.

However, if you stop eating carbohydrates and sugars and get a sufficient portion of your daily energy from fat instead, the body will begin to break that down into ketone bodies. This breakdown of fat is necessary because ketone bodies are more soluble than fats and can cross the blood-brain barrier. This creates an alternative food source to glucose that can be distributed throughout the body to provide it with energy.

You can get into ketosis by fasting because your body burns off all available glycogen over time. Or you can go on a very low-carb, ketogenic diet to induce ketosis. The strongest research recommends limiting carbs to fifty grams per day to keep the body in ketosis. Both ways induce fat loss.

There are a lot of differing opinions regarding the optimal protein-to-fat ratio for a ketogenic diet. However, you don't need any consistent fat intake at all to be on a ketogenic diet because you don't need any calories to go into ketosis, as it can be a result of fasting. You just need to be void of glucose, so you cannot be actively consuming carbohydrates. We recommend focusing on getting the right amount of protein. Whatever fat comes with that food will likely be sufficient.

This addresses one of the largest myths of ketosis. Many internet promoters of "ketogenic nutrition" push the idea that you can eat however much fat you want. This is absolutely false and will not help you with anything except your blood glucose levels. If you eat too much fat too often while on a ketogenic diet, it can still promote obesity and will not help you build muscle. Don't pay any attention to this recommendation. It is wrong, and all you have to do is focus your nutrition on quality protein. This will most likely come along with some fats, which are required but should not be your focus.

Carnivore/Low-Carbohydrate Nutrition

Once we realized this after reading so much bad "ketogenic nutrition" information, it led us to our next conclusion: eating meat only is the easiest way to reach your daily protein requirements. John can easily consume 250 grams of protein in a single meal. He might eat three steaks or a family-sized bucket of chicken minus the skin.

John is often asked about vitamins when he discusses his carnivore diet. In response, he points to two studies. One shows that if you're eating whole foods and your goal is to get to the recommended daily intake of vitamins, you'd need to consume 27,000 calories a day.[121] Clearly, no one ever comes close to that. It's unnecessary and makes it seem as though the standard recommendations were designed to sell vitamins. The other study shows women who took a multivitamin every day had a shorter life expectancy.[122] That doesn't prove multivitamins are harmful, of course, but it certainly isn't evidence that you need to take them. Instead of defaulting to these questionable recommendations, John has been carefully monitoring his own health with respect to his diet and found that he shows no signs of any deficiencies. If anything, he's healthier than ever.

BEING STRONG AND LEAN = A LONGER, MORE DISEASE-FREE LIFE

There is a great deal of conflicting research out there. Some studies indicate certain nutrition programs may lead to longer life spans and others suggest the same programs result in shorter life spans. Other studies show certain types of nutri-

---

121 Calton, J. B. (2010). Prevalence of micronutrient deficiency in popular diet plans. *Journal of the International Society of Sports Nutrition*, *7*(1), 24.

122 Mursu, J., Robien, K., Harnack, L. J., Park, K., & Jacobs, D. R. (2011). Dietary supplements and mortality rate in older women: the Iowa Women's Health Study. *Archives of Internal Medicine*, *171*(18), 1625-1633.

tion decrease one type of cancer risk while increasing the risk of another type.[123] So we asked ourselves a few questions:

- If people are using our variable-resistance product and their primary objective is gaining muscle mass, what would be the optimized nutrition program for them?
- Others who use the product may be divided in their objectives—meaning optimizing body composition but also maximizing their quality and the length of life. So what nutrition principles would be optimized for quality and length of life?

Our top objective in determining what recommendations to make was to cut through the conflicting research to identify indicators with no conflicting research that were associated with better all-cause mortality rates. We identified two: higher levels of physical strength and lower levels of body fat. Researchers have concluded, "Mortality rates were lower for individuals with moderate/high muscular fitness compared to individuals with low muscular fitness."[124] This conclusion has been supported by more clinical data,[125,126] the most telling of which was presented in the Honolulu Longevity study. In this, people in the highest

---

123 Key, T. J., Appleby, P. N., Spencer, E. A., Travis, R. C., Roddam, A. W., & Allen, N. E. (2009). Cancer incidence in vegetarians: results from the European Prospective Investigation into Cancer and Nutrition (EPIC-Oxford). *The American Journal of Clinical Nutrition, 89*(5), 1620S-1626S.

124 FitzGerald, S. J., Barlow, C. E., Kampert, J. B., Morrow, J. R., Jackson, A. W., & Blair, S. N. (2004). Muscular fitness and all-cause mortality: prospective observations. *Journal of Physical Activity and Health, 1*(1), 7-18.

125 Metter, E. J., Talbot, L. A., Schrager, M., & Conwit, R. (2002). Skeletal muscle strength as a predictor of all-cause mortality in healthy men. *The Journals of Gerontology Series A: Biological Sciences and Medical Sciences, 57*(10), B359-B365.

126 Artero, E. G., Lee, D. C., Ruiz, J. R., Sui, X., Ortega, F. B., Church, T. S., ...& Blair, S. N. (2011). A prospective study of muscular strength and all-cause mortality in men with hypertension. *Journal of the American College of Cardiology, 57*(18), 1831-1837.

quartile for strength (lean muscle mass) showed a 250 percent increased chance of living until one hundred years old.[127]

Studies with leaner test subjects demonstrate improved all-cause mortality, but unfortunately, these have been more difficult to understand based on the exact measures used for evaluation. For example, body mass index has been a standard of measure of conditioning for the last fifteen years. The problem with this metric is it takes no aspect of muscularity into consideration. So, in studies of individuals who are involved in strength-type exercise, this metric does not differentiate between those who are muscular and those who are obese. This can lead to misleading conclusions being made "showing" that higher body mass index individuals were at times healthier.

More recently, researchers have begun to focus more on body composition as measured by DEXA scans, caliper measurements, and even waist circumference, which has been shown to be significantly more accurate.[128] Now that more relevant metrics are being used, it is becoming clear that individuals with a lower percentage of body fat live longer. Research has positively identified "the importance of waist circumference as a risk factor for mortality in older adults, regardless of body mass index."

Once we confirmed higher levels of strength and lower levels of percentage body fat are drivers of a longer life and found no conflicting research, the next question was, "What nutritional

127 Rantanen, T., Masaki, K., He, Q., Ross, G. W., Willcox, B. J., & White, L. (2012). Midlife muscle strength and human longevity up to age 100 years: a 44-year prospective study among a decedent cohort. *Age, 34*(3), 563-570.

128 Jacobs, E. J., Newton, C. C., Wang, Y., Patel, A. V., McCullough, M. L., Campbell, P. T., & Gapstur, S. M. (2010). Waist circumference and all-cause mortality in a large US cohort. *Archives of Internal Medicine, 170*(15), 1293-1301.

principles should be adopted so that we can optimize these two metrics?"

When we first launched the X3 product, we wanted to make sure that everyone got the most out of their experience. John had been triggering ketogenesis for thirteen years by then, so that was the default recommendation. As time progressed, we realized the need to continually challenge our recommendations based on the latest research. But we also knew that we were unique insofar as our primary goal was for people to be successful with our physical medicine/X3 product. We hadn't previously recommended a nutritional product, therefore we had no conflict of interest. John said at the time, "If research shows vegan nutrition drives high levels of muscularity and low levels of body fat at the same time, then that's what we'll recommend."

It quickly became apparent to us that the majority of the human diet should come from protein. What's more, our recommendation of one gram per pound of body weight per day (2.2 g/kilogram) doesn't leave room in the intestines for much more—especially when we factor in the option of time-restricted-eating windows, another one of those few nutritional principles that has little to no conflicting research. We already knew protein quality is not the same, and that most vegetable-based proteins or protein products have a single-digit percentage of usability compared with steak at 38 percent usability or eggs at 48 percent usability.[129,130] The way to maximize muscularity while getting as lean as possible through nutrition became obvious: eat high

129 Lucà-Moretti, M. (1998). A Comparative, Double-blind, Triple Crossover Net Nitrogen Utilization Study Confirms the Discovery of the Master Amino Acid Pattern. *Age (years)*, *152*(176), 41-5.

130 Hoffman, J. R., & Falvo, M. J. (2004). Protein–which is best? *Journal of Sports Science & Medicine*, *3*(3), 118.

levels of animal proteins that offer the potential for even higher quality essential amino acid complexes.

There are smartphone applications, web interfaces, and even computer client-side software you can use to count calories and macronutrients—and none of them that we have tested are accurate. The way in which calories and macronutrients are used within the body depends on a variety of factors and is not easily measured. For example, brain activity may be higher or lower based on how an individual spends their day. But it's not like reading a technical journal has some sort of caloric value—it may require more or less brain activity depending on the individual. The majority of people who use caloric intake trackers feel they do worse and end up with more body fat. In fact, in a My Fitness Pal study conducted with individuals suffering from eating disorders, researchers concluded, "73% of these users perceived the app as contributing to their eating disorder. Furthermore, we found that these perceptions were correlated with eating disorder symptoms."[131]

We've already cited literature demonstrating time-restricted-eating windows, even with the same caloric daily total intake as ordinary eating patterns, preserve more muscle while decreasing body fat. We've also cited research showing the hormonal differences optimizing the loss of body fat in these periods of time. But even beyond that, a calorie is still not a calorie when it comes to body fat. The fact is protein overfeeding does not result in fat storage but rather in thermogenesis, where body temperature increases to metabolize protein. Fat storage

---

131 Levinson, C. A., Fewell, L., & Brosof, L. C. (2017). My Fitness Pal calorie tracker usage in the eating disorders. *Eating Behaviors*, *27*, 14-16.

comes from consuming too many calories of dietary fats and carbohydrates.[132]

In other words, only the fats or the carbohydrates you eat are stored as body fat, even when you are at a calorie surplus. Excess protein your body cannot use seems to contribute to increasing your body temperature and enables you to use the energy while digesting.

When considering how we came to these conclusions and the order in which we discovered the pertinent research, we had no bias in this project. We just wanted to give X3 users the best nutritional information we could find. There was no financial motivation. There wasn't even any confirmation bias because of something we had already been doing.

As we were on this journey, we came across Dr. Shawn Baker who was just getting ready to be on the Joe Rogan podcast. While his presentation on why someone would want to be eating primarily animal proteins was different, the conclusion was the same and added reinforcement to the nutrition recommendations we had grown to support and enact in our approach to nutrition.

DO WE "CHERRY-PICK" NUTRITION RESEARCH?

Internet commenters often claim certain research is "cherry-picked." Cherry-picking is an abuse of research in which someone points out evidence that supports their claim while ignoring the evidence against their claim. On some occasions

132 Bray, G. A., Redman, L. M., de Jonge, L., Covington, J., Rood, J., Brock, C., ...& Smith, S. R. (2015). Effect of protein overfeeding on energy expenditure measured in a metabolic chamber. *The American Journal of Clinical Nutrition, 101*(3), 496-505.

this is a real concern—say when someone is intentionally misleading an audience by choosing research citations that are already heavily biased or even omitting certain key details.

Cherry-picking data happens almost every presidential election cycle. Let's take unemployment numbers as an example. If an analyst wants to make a president look good, they choose a starting date when unemployment was terrible and an end point when unemployment was improved, giving the impression that the president saved the economy. But they just as easily can make the opposite look true by cherry-picking data with a different time frame.

Every physiology study asks a research question and then presents data related to mechanisms in the human body. They may even try to drive attention to future potential discoveries, so the next research studies gain support and ask more specific questions. Selecting one piece of data from a study and omitting other more important pieces that contribute to the conclusion can also constitute cherry-picking.

We do not cherry-pick. However, we do look for unbiased studies in the nutrition industry that uphold our nutritional recommendations. Some critics would call this cherry-picking, but it really isn't. The subject of nutritional research cannot be fully discussed without addressing the financial interests of the food industry—and by "food" we especially mean the packaged, processed, high-margin food-like substances that line so many grocery store shelves.

SCIENCE-BACKED, UNBIASED NUTRITION CONCLUSIONS

In the book *Unsavory Truth: How Food Companies Skew the Science of What We Eat*, Marion Nestle, Professor of Nutrition Emeritus, Food Studies and Public Health at New York University, states, "Pomegranates might have high antioxidant activity," and then she asks, "Compared to what?" The fact is, as Dr. Nestle's book explains, the people advertising the fruit don't care about the question. Their only goal, and the goal of most company-sponsored studies, is to make more money. "It's marketing research, not science."[133]

The pharmaceutical industry is no different from the food product industry in terms of bias and sponsorship, as detailed in a recent *New York Times* article. In September 2018, the director of clinical research at the Memorial Sloan Kettering Cancer Center relinquished his post after failing to disclose financial conflicts of interest from pharmaceutical companies, for whom he had done research and from whom he had received millions of dollars in compensation. An investigation revealed he had altered the data to favor the drug being tested.[134] There is actually scientific research on this sort of bias. A 2007 meta-analysis published in the *BMJ* showed that for research on antihypertensive drugs. "Although financial ties to one drug company were not associated with favorable results, such ties constituted the only characteristic significantly associated with favorable conclusions (4.09, 1.30 to 12.83). When controlling for other characteristics of meta-analyses in multiple logistic regression analyses, meta-analyses that had financial ties to

133 Nestle, M. (2018). Unsavory truth: how food companies skew the science of what we eat. Basic Books.

134 Brody, J. E. (2018). Confused by Nutrition Research? Sloppy Science May Be to Blame. Retrieved January 29, 2020, from https://www.nytimes.com/2018/10/29/well/live/confused-by-nutrition-research-sloppy-science-may-be-to-blame.amp.html.

one drug company remained more likely to report favorable conclusions (5.11, 1.54 to 16.92)."[135] The good news is that the results did not skew favorably due to funding, meaning that there was no evidence that the researchers actually tampered with data, which would be truly malevolent. However, a strong correlation between positive conclusions and funding sources did exist and this suggests that researchers "spin" the data to support the people paying them. Given the psychology around "gifts" and the concept of reciprocity, the researchers may not be doing this intentionally (i.e., it may be subconscious), but nonetheless this effect is quite pernicious since many people do not examine the actual raw data on any given study.

Perhaps the most egregious nutritional recommendation most of you will remember is "breakfast is the most important meal of the day." This idea was invented in the nineteenth century by Seventh Day Adventists' James Caleb Jackson and John Harvey Kellogg to sell their newly invented breakfast cereal.[136] There is not a single study that supports this idea. Absolutely none.

Now that we have given you some background in nutritional research, the following is a list of conclusions from studies not funded by food companies, religious groups like Seventh-day Adventists that believe forcing vegetarian nutrition on the entire population is their God-given mandate, or even the potentially biased meat-production industry:

- Neither red, processed, or white meat consumption are

---

135 Yank, V., Rennie, D., & Bero, L. A. (2007). Financial ties and concordance between results and conclusions in meta-analyses: retrospective cohort study. *BMJ*, 335(7631), 1202-1205.

136 Klein, S. (2017). A Brief History Of How Breakfast Got Its 'Healthy' Rep. Retrieved January 29, 2020, from https://www.huffpost.com/entry/breakfast-most-important-history_n_5910054.

consistently associated with all-cause or cause-specific mortality.[137]

- Vegetarians have no mortality advantage over meat-eaters.[138] In fact, a vegetarian diet is associated with poorer health (higher incidences of cancer, allergies, and mental health disorders), a higher need for healthcare, and poorer quality of life.[139] Another study concludes, "We found no evidence that following a vegetarian diet, semi-vegetarian diet or a pesco-vegetarian diet has an independent protective effect on all-cause mortality."[140]
- A study of forty-two European countries found lower cardiovascular disease and mortality among countries that consumed more fats and meats. Higher cardiovascular mortality was linked to carbohydrate consumption.[141]
- Plant-based diets are indicated for causing bone density loss, NOT helping it: "The findings gathered consistently support the hypothesis that vegans do have lower bone mineral density than their non-vegan counterparts." The researchers go on to say that science is not clear if the issue is calcium plus

---

137 Kappeler, R., Eichholzer, M., & Rohrmann, S. (2013). Meat consumption and diet quality and mortality in NHANES III. *European Journal of Clinical Nutrition*, 67(6), 598.

138 Key, T. J., Appleby, P. N., Spencer, E. A., Travis, R. C., Roddam, A. W., & Allen, N. E. (2009). Mortality in British vegetarians: results from the European Prospective Investigation into Cancer and Nutrition (EPIC-Oxford). The American *Journal of Clinical Nutrition*, 89(5), 1613S-1619S.

139 Burkert, N. T., Muckenhuber, J., Großschädl, F., Rásky, E., & Freidl, W. (2014). Nutrition and health–the association between eating behavior and various health parameters: a matched sample study. PloS One, 9(2), e88278.

140 Mihrshahi, S., Ding, D., Gale, J., Allman-Farinelli, M., Banks, E., & Bauman, A. E. (2017). Vegetarian diet and all-cause mortality: Evidence from a large population-based Australian cohort-the 45 and Up Study. *Preventive Medicine, 97, 1-7.*

141 *Grasgruber, P., Sebera, M.,* Hrazdira, E., Hrebickova, S., & Cacek, J. (2016). Food consumption and the actual statistics of cardiovascular diseases: an epidemiological comparison of 42 European countries. *Food & Nutrition Research*, 60(1), 31694.

vitamin D or if it's another factor, such as protein or even muscular performance.[142]

- Data indicate, "when soy protein is substituted for meat protein, there is an acute decline in dietary calcium bioavailability."[143]
- Twenty studies comprising 37,134 participants showed that "compared with omnivores, vegetarians and vegans had lower BMD at the femoral neck and lumbar spine and vegans also had higher fracture rates."[144]
- Five randomized, controlled trials included in a meta-analysis revealed, "cholesterol lowering interventions showed no evidence of benefit on mortality from coronary heart disease (1.13, 0.83 to 1.54) or all-cause mortality (1.07, 0.90 to 1.27)."[145]
- A twelve-study meta-analysis concluded there is no relationship between protein consumption and kidney function.[146] In fact, there has never been any scientific evidence showing higher protein consumption damages kidney function. Not a single study. Picked up by the mainstream media, this hypothesis has been disproven multiple times, yet the myth unfortunately still persists.

---

142 Smith, A. M. (2006). Veganism and osteoporosis: a review of the current literature. *International Journal of Nursing Practice*, 12(5), 302-306.

143 Kerstetter, J. E., Wall, D. E., O'Brien, K. O., Caseria, D. M., & Insogna, K. L. (2006). Meat and soy protein affect calcium homeostasis in healthy women. *The Journal of Nutrition*, 136(7), 1890-1895.

144 Iguacel, I., Miguel-Berges, M. L., Gómez-Bruton, A., Moreno, L. A., & Julián, C. (2019). Veganism, vegetarianism, bone mineral density, and fracture risk: a systematic review and meta-analysis. Nutrition reviews, 77(1), 1-18.

145 Ramsden, C. E., Zamora, D., Majchrzak-Hong, S., Faurot, K. R., Broste, S. K., Frantz, R. P., ...& Hibbeln, J. R. (2016). Re-evaluation of the traditional diet-heart hypothesis: analysis of recovered data from Minnesota Coronary Experiment (1968-73). *BMJ*, 353, i1246.

146 Devries, M. C., Sithamparapillai, A., Brimble, K. S., Banfield, L., Morton, R. W., & Phillips, S. M. (2018). Changes in kidney function do not differ between healthy adults consuming higher-compared with lower-or normal-protein diets: a systematic review and meta-analysis. *The Journal of Nutrition*, 148(11), 1760-1775.

- Humans have always been carnivores. Researchers conclude, "anthropological evidence from cranio-dental features and fossil stable isotope analysis indicates a growing reliance on meat consumption during human evolution," and "We developed a larger brain balanced by a smaller, simpler gastrointestinal tract requiring higher-quality foods based around meat protein and fat."[147]
- Lower LDL does NOT equal lower risks. "The lowest LDL-C group (LDL< 70 mg/dL) had a higher risk of all-cause mortality (HR 1.95, 1.55–2.47), CVD mortality (HR 2.02, 1.11–3.64), and cancer mortality (HR 2.06, 1.46–2.90) compared to the reference group (LDL 120–139 mg/dL)."[148]
- A meta-analysis of prospective epidemiologic studies showed "there is no significant evidence for concluding that dietary saturated fat is associated with an increased risk of CHD or CVD."[149]
- "Extensive research did not show evidence to support a role of dietary cholesterol in the development of CVD. As a result, the 2015–2020 Dietary Guidelines for Americans (U.S. Department of Health and Human Services) removed the recommendations of restricting dietary cholesterol to 300 mg/day."[150]
- Adolescents who consumed a vegan diet up to the age of six years (even if this diet was stopped) and had an absence

---

147 Mann, N. (2007). Meat in the human diet: An anthropological perspective. *Nutrition & Dietetics*, 64, S102-S107.

148 Sung, K. C., Huh, J. H., Ryu, S., Lee, J. Y., Scorletti, E., Byrne, C. D., ... & Ko, S. B. (2019). Low Levels of Low-Density Lipoprotein Cholesterol and Mortality Outcomes in Non-Statin Users. *Journal of Clinical Medicine*, 8(10), 1571.

149 Siri-Tarino, P. W., Sun, Q., Hu, F. B., & Krauss, R. M. (2010). Meta-analysis of prospective cohort studies evaluating the association of saturated fat with cardiovascular disease. *The American Journal of Clinical Nutrition*, 91(3), 535-546.

150 Soliman, G. (2018). Dietary cholesterol and the lack of evidence in cardiovascular disease. *Nutrients*, 10(6), 780.

of cobalamin (vitamin B12), commonly found in animal-based foods, during their youth showed signs of permanent impaired cognitive function.[151]

- Research shows that "Vitamin D deficiency mainly occurs if a strict vegetarian diet is followed as mostly the source of vitamin D is animal based." Further, "Vitamin D deficiency is directly linked with severe complications in mothers and neonates, causing rickets, poor fetal growth, and infantile eczema in neonates."[152]
- Humans in Western countries consuming a diet of 70 percent plant-based calories also have 70 percent of adults suffering pre-diabetes or T2 diabetes. This rate is even greater in India, which has the highest rate of vegetarians, and where T2 diabetes is even more prevalent.[153]
- "The traditional starch-based diets of some developing nations have likely contributed to the rising risk of chronic disease."[154]
- Vegan and plant-based diets worsen brain health. "This is now more important than ever given that accelerated food trends towards plant-based diets/veganism could have further ramifications on choline intake/status."
- "American Academy of Pediatrics (from 2018) called on pediatricians to move beyond simply recommending a "good diet" and to make sure that pregnant women and young children have access to food that provides adequate amounts

---

151 Louwman, M. W., van Dusseldorp, M., van de Vijver, F. J., Thomas, C. M., Schneede, J., Ueland, P. M., ...& van Staveren, W. A. (2000). Signs of impaired cognitive function in adolescents with marginal cobalamin status. *The American Journal of Clinical Nutrition*, 72(3), 762-769.

152 Elsori, D. H., & Hammoud, M. S. (2018). Vitamin D deficiency in mothers, neonates and children. *The Journal of Steroid Biochemistry and Molecular Biology*, 175, 195-199.

153 Tuso, P. J., Ismail, M. H., Ha, B. P., & Bartolotto, C. (2013). Nutritional update for physicians: plant-based diets. *The Permanente Journal*, 17(2), 61.

154 Ludwig, D. S., Hu, F. B., Tappy, L., & Brand-Miller, J. (2018). Dietary carbohydrates: Role of quality and quantity in chronic disease. *BMJ*, 361, k2340.

of "brain-building" nutrients with choline being listed as one of these."[155]

- Phytoestrogen, also called "dietary estrogen," is a plant-derived estrogen not generated within the endocrine system and consumed by eating phytoestrogenic plants. These are a diverse group of naturally occurring nonsteroidal plant compounds that, because of structural similarity with estradiol (17-β-estradiol), have the ability to cause estrogenic and/or antiestrogenic effects.[156]
- Hypogonadism and erectile dysfunction are also associated with soy product consumption.[157]
- Fourteen days of soy protein supplementation appears to partially blunt serum testosterone.[158]

SCIENCE AND VEGETARIANISM

Nutrition is a fragmented field. There are all kinds of people making all kinds of claims about what's healthy and what's not. In doing research, we found science favors a carnivore diet. If it had shown vegan nutrition was optimal for performance, that would be our recommendation, but it has not. Keep in mind, the current Western diet is 70 percent plant-based.[159] We are fatter and sicker than ever, so why would going 80 percent or 90 percent plant-based help?

---

155 Derbyshire, E. (2019). Could we be overlooking a potential choline crisis in the United Kingdom?. *BMJ Nutrition, Prevention & Health*, bmjnph-2019.

156 Yildiz F (2005). *Phytoestrogens in Functional Foods*. Taylor & Francis Ltd. pp. 3–5, 210–211.

157 Siepmann, T., Roofeh, J., Kiefer, F. W., & Edelson, D. G. (2011). Hypogonadism and erectile dysfunction associated with soy product consumption. *Nutrition*, 27(7-8), 859-862.

158 Kraemer, W. J., Solomon-Hill, G., Volk, B. M., Kupchak, B. R., Looney, D. P., Dunn-Lewis, C., ...& Maresh, C. M. (2013). The effects of soy and whey protein supplementation on acute hormonal responses to resistance exercise in men. *Journal of the American College of Nutrition*, 32(1), 66-74.

159 Tuso, P. J., Ismail, M. H., Ha, B. P., & Bartolotto, C. (2013). Nutritional update for physicians: plant-based diets. *The Permanente Journal*, 17(2), 61.

You can live on veganism. It won't kill you, although you increase the risk of malnutrition issues. However, if you're just watching television or sitting at a desk every day, like many people, your diet may not be the main factor limiting your physical potential.

While there are no toxins in meat, plants produce their own toxins called oxalates. The way an animal keeps you from eating it is by running away. The way a plant keeps you from eating it is by poisoning you.

Some oxalates create more sensitivity than others. Ultimately, they come together to form glyoxylate, a concentration of different plant toxins. For example, nightshade plants like tomatoes, potatoes, and eggplants contain toxins that cause inflammation.[160] The entire reason people take antioxidants is because they are oxidizing, or becoming inflamed. When you cut out toxin-filled plants, you'll no longer experience inflammation from these substances, and many studies have suggested inflammation is the driver of multiple chronic diseases involving the nervous system, immune system, and brain impairment.[161]

It is also very difficult to meet the daily protein requirement we recommend while eating a vegetarian diet. Technically, there's protein in broccoli but would it be physically possible to consume enough broccoli to hit that number? For example, to get to one hundred grams of protein, you would need to eat at least eight pounds of broccoli.

---

160 Prenen, J. A., Boer, P., & Dorhout Mees, E. J. (1984). Absorption kinetics of oxalate from oxalate-rich food in man. *The American Journal of Clinical Nutrition*, *40*(5), 1007-1010.

161 Vida, C., M Gonzalez, E., & De la Fuente, M. (2014). Increase of oxidation and inflammation in nervous and immune systems with aging and anxiety. *Current Pharmaceutical Design*, *20*(29), 4656-4678.

IF YOU CHOOSE TO BE VEGAN DESPITE THE MALNUTRITION DANGERS

We understand there are people of conviction who will stick to veganism or vegetarianism no matter what. While we are presenting science that encourages moving away from this, we would rather help those who are going to stick to it than not. Aside from the unavailability of vitamin B12 from any plant source, the biggest problem plant-based people have is much more limited options to consume enough quality protein.

As shown earlier, plant-based sources are not usable by the body, with the exception of single-digit percentages by volume, so this is a particular challenge for vegans. Vegetarians have access to egg, the most usable of all naturally occurring proteins, and to cheese, which is reasonably usable for a naturally occurring protein. For vegetarians who are tired of eating lots of eggs, and for vegans, we recommend supplementing with Fortagen. Each serving can be counted as 50g towards your target protein intake, so this can really move the needle.

We wanted Fortagen to be available to everyone, so it contains no animal-derived ingredients, and the fermentation-based production process also involves no animals. It's worth noting that many plant-based dieters work hard to meet protein intake minimums and succeed, but those minimums are almost always based on outdated guidelines. It is much more challenging to reach the 1g of protein per pound of body weight guideline we have found to be supported by research (as previously outlined in this book).

One myth on this subject that persists in vegan discussions is that broccoli, for example, has as much protein as steak. This is often perpetuated by infographics comparing protein per calorie. Many are simply inaccurate, but even the correct statistics can be misleading when presented in this way. For example, one hundred calories of broccoli have eight grams of protein. That same number of calories of New York steak has 13.6g of protein. Steak still has far more, but the numbers may seem surprisingly close for "similar servings." The problem is, those aren't similar serving sizes—it is over ten ounces of broccoli and just two ounces of steak.

Consider how this creates a problem for a 200-pound person who wants to gain muscle and is using broccoli as the main protein source, as many Facebook posts seem to suggest is possible. From the previous numbers, we can calculate that there are thirteen grams of protein in one pound of broccoli and 109 grams of protein in one pound of steak. For our hypothetical individual to get to 200 grams of protein (one gram per pound of body weight as required to optimally grow muscle), this means they would have to consume over fifteen pounds of broccoli just to get to the gram requirement, versus less than two pounds of steak—and this isn't even fully fair to the steak, since it has higher percent protein usability as we discussed in the protein section.

These extremely high food consumption requirements compare proportionally to the amount of plant material a gorilla eats per day, which explains how they can have so much muscle mass. Unfortunately, it's just not possible for humans to eat this amount of plant matter on a daily basis. As mentioned before, we believe protein intake is key, and vegans and vegetarians should be mindful of the quality and usability of the protein they consume and also of the disparity between "standard guidelines" for protein consumption (which are woefully low) and the amount of protein consumption that research suggests is actually optimal for human performance.

CHAPTER 7

FALSEHOODS OF FITNESS

By now, you may be wondering which other fitness "facts" you put your faith in are actually false. The sheer number of exercise principles that fall under this umbrella will probably astound you. It certainly astounded us.

You see, we didn't set out to investigate any of the following myths. In fact, we weren't even aware of some of them until they were brought to our attention on the X3 social media pages. In certain cases, people commenting there felt compelled to educate us about these "facts," while other times they were reaching out to ask us if a given piece of exercise advice was true.

In either event, we dug into the research to get to the bottom of the issues. We were committed to making the best possible exercise recommendations. That meant understanding the research supporting—and more often discounting—fitness concepts people had learned at the gym.

Whether they made their way into the fitness world through initial misinterpretation of research, personal anecdotes, or were simply fabricated at some point by somebody wanting to be seen as an expert, these mistaken beliefs are definitely not helping your workout. In fact, they are probably holding you back from reaching your goals. In this chapter, we aim to set the record straight with science.

FALSEHOOD #1: CARDIO IS HEALTHIER THAN STRENGTH TRAINING

This is the belief cardio is the only kind of exercise that provides real longevity benefits, whereas strength training is optional, supplemental, or perhaps only important in the context of vanity. Effectively people are saying, "Strength training is fine, but you need to do cardio to be healthy."

In our experience, people using the word "cardio" in this way are referring to endurance aerobic activities like spending hours on the elliptical or running long distances, without the inclusion of a strength training component. Using the term "cardio" to describe this type of exercise is quite misleading. First, all exercise is cardiovascular, meaning it imposes demands on the heart. But more importantly, when it comes to cardiac health, weight training provides the same, if not more cardiovascular benefits compared to strictly "cardio" exercise.

Cardio is also a suboptimal protocol for achieving your health and fitness goals—it may even make them more difficult to achieve. In one experiment, patients with Type 2 diabetes in a group assigned to perform strength training saw improved blood lipid profiles and glycemic control while the group assigned to "cardio" exercise saw no statistically significant improvements in these metrics.[162] Other research shows strength training improves endothelial function, an important component of cardiac health,[163,164] and can effectively lower blood pressure.[165] In addition, a meta-analysis of more than one hundred studies concluded strength training provides equivalent cardiovascular fitness improvement to traditional "cardio" exercise, and this benefit primarily correlated with the intensity of the exercise rather than duration.[166]

To be clear, when we say "cardio" isn't necessary, we don't mean that you shouldn't care about your cardiovascular fitness. You should care, and so do we. But when you evaluate the evidence, it shows strength training provides all the cardiac benefit people currently associate with long-distance running or hours on the elliptical. In addition, strength training offers the benefit of substantial added musculature, which keeps the heart working more efficiently at all times in order to meet the additional demand for circulation imposed by that tissue.

Unfortunately, the cardiac benefits of this exercise type unfortunately diminish quickly if you take a break from it.

---

162 Cauza, E., Hanusch-Enserer, U., Strasser, B., Ludvik, B., Metz-Schimmerl, S., Pacini, G., …& Dunky, A. (2005). The relative benefits of endurance and strength training on the metabolic factors and muscle function of people with Type 2 diabetes mellitus. *Archives of Physical Medicine and Rehabilitation, 86*(8), 1527-1533.

163 Olson, T. P., Dengel, D. R., Leon, A. S., & Schmitz, K. H. (2006). Moderate resistance training and vascular health in overweight women. *Medicine & Science in Sports & Exercise, 38*(9), 1558-1564.

164 Rakobowchuk, M., McGowan, C. L., De Groot, P. C., Hartman, J. W., Phillips, S. M., & MacDonald, M. J. (2005). Endothelial function of young healthy males following whole body resistance training. *Journal of Applied Physiology, 98*(6), 2185-2190.

165 Cornelissen, V. A., & Fagard, R. H. (2005). Effect of resistance training on resting blood pressure: a meta-analysis of randomized, controlled trials.

166 Steele, J., Fisher, J., & Bruce-Low, S. (2012). Resistance training to momentary muscular failure improves cardiovascular fitness in humans: a review of acute physiological responses and chronic physiological adaptations. *Journal of Exercise Physiology Online, 15*(3), 53-80.

Cardiovascular endurance—in other words, your aerobic fitness—begins to decline just seven days after you stop working out. Structural fitness, or your body's ability to withstand the impact of stressful cardio activities, is lost almost as fast.

For example, let's say you're a great runner. You successfully complete a marathon, averaging six minutes per mile. You then take half a year off of training before deciding to go run another marathon. This time, you are disappointed to find your six-minute-mile pace has fallen into the ten-minute-per-mile range. What happened? While you still have the capacity to be an accomplished athlete, your cardiovascular endurance began deteriorating right after you finished that first marathon. Your body sought homeostasis, and you no longer have the heart of a marathon runner. Now you have to start over almost from scratch.

FALSEHOOD #2: THERE IS ONE SUPERIOR METHOD FOR TESTING BODY FAT

Ultimately, what most of us want is to look fantastic when we see ourselves in the mirror. For that reason, we typically look at percentage of fat as a way to measure lean body mass—the lower, the better.

There are multiple ways of testing body fat. None of them are "wrong," but they will likely give you a different result. Knowing how each method works may help you track your progress more effectively. The most important thing is to pick a testing method and stick with it.

DEXA scans provide a true measure of fat versus lean mass (muscle, bone, organs, and skin) percentage. Body fat tends to register 4 percent higher with DEXA scans than with calipers (as reported in three cross-sectional National Health and Nutrition Examination Survey studies conducted from 1999–2004), much to the frustration of athletes.[167,168] This is because DEXA scans are not just pinching the body fat in aesthetically advantageous areas like calipers do, but measuring it in your hands, feet, and other places where it is almost impossible to lose fat (and where you wouldn't want to lose fat anyway) because it exists there to protect your bones, tendons, ligaments, and muscles.

Bioimpedance is another body fat measurement method. It puts electrical signals through different limbs and measures the resulting conductivity. Fat is a better conductor than muscle or bone, so it takes a metric from the conductive signaling to determine the percentage of body fat you have. Unfortunately, hydration seems to skew the results more than with any other method, and nobody is hydrated exactly the same way every day. This means significant variability in body composition test results from this method may be attributable to your level of hydration rather than actual changes in body fat percentage.

Recently, we've been reading research on a body fat testing calculation that simply uses the circumferences of certain body parts. For example, male subjects provide a neck measurement from just below the larynx and a waist measurement in line with the naval. This test is easy to perform and repeat, with results showing a strong level of congruency with DEXA scans.[169] Also,

167 Laurson, K. R., Eisenmann, J. C., & Welk, G. J. (2011). Body fat percentile curves for US children and adolescents. *American Journal of Preventive Medicine*, 41(4), S87-S92.

168 Borrud, L. G., Flegal, K. M., Freedman, D. S., Li, Y., & Ogden, C. L. (2011). Smoothed percentage body fat percentiles for US children and adolescents, 1999-2004, https://stacks.cdc.gov/view/cdc/13173/Print.

169 Combest, T. M., Howard, R. S., & Andrews, A. M. (2017). Comparison of Circumference Body Composition Measurements and Eight-Point Bioelectrical Impedance Analysis to Dual Energy X-Ray Absorptiometry to Measure Body Fat Percentage. *Military Medicine*, 182(7), e1908-e1912.

hydration does not skew this test (unless someone drinks sixty-plus ounces of water and it makes their stomach/midsection appear and measure larger in circumference). To avoid that kind of influence, this would be a great measurement to take first thing in the morning after urinating.

Again, none of these tests are perfect. Whether you decide to use calipers, DEXA scanning, bioimpedance, or circumference measurements, we simply suggest choosing one method and sticking to it to ensure you are getting consistent data with which to track your progress.

FALSEHOOD #3: CARDIO IS GREAT FOR WEIGHT LOSS

Research shows prolonged cardio—logging long runs, for example—is an ineffective means to lose weight. By upregulating cortisol, the body's stress hormone, cardio can have the complete opposite effect of what you're trying to accomplish. It actually can contribute to your body holding on to the kind of "stubborn fat" so many people have trouble losing with traditional exercise routines.

Prolonged cardio breaks down muscle tissue rather than building it.[170] This is why long-term marathon runners often look thin, saggy, and have an exaggerated kyphotic curve. They've amassed thousands of hours of training but never developed any muscle while doing it, and in many cases, the muscle they do have is damaged.

The one thing cardio can do very effectively is produce chronic

170 Peeters, G. M. E. E., Van Schoor, N. M., Van Rossum, E. F. C., Visser, M., & Lips, P. T. A. M. (2008). The relationship between cortisol, muscle mass and muscle strength in older persons and the role of genetic variations in the glucocorticoid receptor. *Clinical Endocrinology*, 69(4), 673-682.

joint damage. The repetitive impact caused by long-distance running, for example, puts stress on the joint and compromises joint positions. This combined with the added strain of not giving the body time to recover between long runs adds up over time. This may sound surprising, but there is scientific research on the subject. When comparing a quadriceps biopsy of a distance runner with a sprinter's, the marathoner's muscle shows significant cell damage whereas the sprinter's does not.[171]

So if you want to be a long-distance runner or bike the Tour de France, by all means, have at it. Do it for the fun and adventure. But just realize that this is not an optimal path if you aim to be healthier and thinner, with any significant muscle development or definition. And, compared to or combined with strength training, it may actually be counterproductive to you achieving those sorts of fitness goals.

FALSEHOOD #4: MUSCLE CONFUSION THEORY/ MUSCLE DAMAGE IS REQUIRED FOR GROWTH

Muscle confusion theory is the idea that you have to constantly change your workout to keep getting muscular gains. This concept rests on the idea that you need to "confuse" your muscle tissue regularly to keep your body from "adapting" to your exercise regimen, whereupon it would allegedly stop responding to it. Muscle confusion theory is a driving force behind complicated fitness fads such as P90X, Bodypump, and ClassPass. This idea was promoted in the past by one of the most famous bodybuilder-actor-politicians, who may be the ultimate origin of the myth.

---

171 Sjöström M, Johansson C, Lorentzon R. (1988). Muscle pathology in m. quadriceps of marathon runners. Early signs of strain disease or functional adaptation? *Acta Physiol Scanda*, 132(4): 537-41.

The main result of applying muscle confusion theory to fitness seems to be muscle soreness. Many people believe muscle soreness is the sign of a good workout and impending muscle growth, but it is actually indicative of muscle damage. Contrary to popular belief, soreness is not required to facilitate muscle growth and may stop it from happening altogether.

There is no good evidence to support muscle damage as a requirement (or even being helpful) in spurring strength gains or muscle hypertrophy. The best research on this subject, conducted in 2018, concluded, "muscle damage is not the process that mediates or potentiates RT-induced muscle hypertrophy."[172] What's more, this same research suggests hypertrophy only occurs after muscle tissue completes damage attenuation from a workout, and true growth is more pronounced when muscle damage is minimal. In other words, the more damage you create, the less muscle growth you experience. Muscle damage doesn't do anything except compromise your body and delay the onset of muscle protein synthesis associated with real hypertrophy.

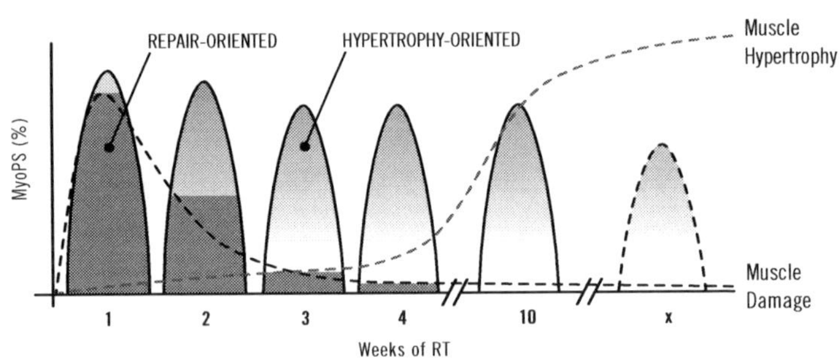

Besides, if you're always trying a new workout, you're always learning a new form and getting used to new movements. This

172 Damas F, Libardi CA, Ugrinowitsch C. (2018). The development of skeletal hypertrophy through resistance training: the role of muscle damage and muscle protein synthesis. *Eur J Appl Physiol.* 118(3): 485-500.

is likely to detract from the actual intensity of your efforts. It also makes you more prone to injury because you are more likely to be doing new exercises incorrectly compared to exercises you have practiced before.

This might also be why the myth still exists. If you begin to routinely cycle through new exercises, you're likely to see rep count gains early on simply because you're learning to do the exercise properly and becoming more accustomed to the movement. People seeing these rapid "gains" might mistakenly attribute them to a period of rapid growth in response to the muscle tissue being "confused." This, of course, is not true. If you track your muscle growth using DEXA scans or other metrics, you'll get a much more accurate insight into exercise efficacy.

Another reason people believe this myth is it gives them an excuse to change up their workout to avoid boredom. While having a deliberately inconsistent workout routine in the name of muscle confusion theory is likely to diminish your results and increase the risk of injury, you certainly may find the variation "more interesting." But if boredom is a factor, take a step back and think about what you're trying to achieve with your workout. Is it excitement, or muscle gain and fat loss?

Think of it this way: when you're brushing your teeth, the goal is to maintain good hygiene, avoid painful and costly dental procedures, and have nice-looking teeth and fresh breath. Tooth brushing is not exciting, but it gets the results you're seeking. Now if someone suggested you start brushing your teeth with a sock, just to mix things up, would you even consider doing that instead? We don't think so. Even though it might add variety to your routine, it would also be less effective and probably even counterproductive. That's pretty much how we see muscle confusion theory.

Finally, muscle confusion theory has been tested and it turns out people who stick to a consistent exercise routine achieve better results. The American College of Sports Medicine recommends "progressive overload" as the most effective way to post muscle and strength gains.[173] This strength training workout method continually challenges your muscles through increasing resistance, weight, repetitions, or a combination thereof. It is the type of workout X3 gives you.

FALSEHOOD #5: THE WELL-ROUNDED ATHLETE

There's no good reason to set your fitness goal as being a "well-rounded athlete."

Yes, you can pursue and even get good at a plethora of things: running long distances, lifting weights, racing with a rock over your head. However, in comparison to someone who is more specific about their training, you won't be very accomplished at a single one of them, and your training routines will likely interfere with each other and make progress needlessly difficult.

That's because these workouts have conflicting goals. When you do endurance activities, you're upregulating cortisol, which keeps fat on the body and breaks down muscular tissue. When you do strength training, you're downregulating cortisol and

173 Kraemer WJ, Adams K, Cafarelli E, Dudley GA, Dooly C. Feigenbaum MS, Fleck SJ, Franklin B, Fry AC, Hoffman JR, Newton RU, Potteiger J, Stone MH, Ratamess NA, Triplett-McBride T, American College of Sports Medicine. (2002). American College of Sports Medicine position stand. Progression models in resistance training for healthy adults. *Med Sci Sports Exerc*,34(2): 364–80.

upregulating growth hormone, which promotes body fat loss and protects lean tissue.

The combination of these different exercises has an inverse effect of what you want. Hormonally, you're just spinning your wheels. It's as if you drove five feet forward, then five feet backward, and wonder why you're not where you want to be yet.

FALSEHOOD #6: MOST "FACTS" ABOUT MUSCLE FIBER TYPES

This myth includes a lot of variations regarding specific muscle fiber types and the exercise requirements, benefits, and implications of each. Some people have told us, "I have more type one than type two muscle fibers," assuming the distribution based on the exercise method they prefer.

Some people tell us athletic abilities are defined by the percentage of muscle fiber types an individual is born with, and they tell us that ratio can't be changed. Others believe regular strength training benefits only certain types of muscle fibers, and some other kind of exercise is necessary to benefit all muscle tissues.

The first thing you need to realize is—unless you've examined your muscle tissue under a microscope—you almost certainly don't know the percentage of each muscle fiber type you have. You may be good at distance running, but that doesn't prove you have more slow-twitch, endurance-specific muscle fibers. It may just be that you enjoy running, trained hard, and became accomplished at it. Effort and training generally exert far more influence on athletic performance than muscle fiber type breakdown. Consider this: any untrained non-athlete living a sedentary lifestyle still has a specific amount of fast- and slow-twitch muscle, but does it make them particularly good at any athletic endeavor—weightlifting, running, sprinting—as compared to someone who trains for that kind of exercise?

Second, muscle fibers can change when properly stimulated. Research published in the *Journal of Applied Physiology* demonstrated not only can the ratio of type 2A and type 2X muscle fibers change, but the ratio of type one and type two muscle fibers can too, given the right exercise stimulus.[174] Just as eye color is not a determinant of how good of a tennis player you're going to be, the percentages of fiber types you possess are not a determinant of how much muscle you can grow or how long you can run.

Third, science shows regular strength training can grow all muscle fibers; you don't have to worry about which fibers will benefit and which will languish. When it comes to resistance, you're not just working type one or type two muscle fibers in isolation, you're working all of them.

A recent study supports the hypothesis that strength training leads to increases in both types of muscle. At the end of the experiment, total muscle fiber mass had increased but the ratio of fiber types had remained constant, thereby proving that all fiber types had been affected.[175] Further, the training applied to stimulate fast- versus slow-twitch muscle is conflicting. The

---

174 Liu Y, Schlumberger A, Wirth K, Schmidtbleicher D, & Steinacker JM.(2003). Different effects on human skeletal myosin heavy chain isoform expression: strength vs. combination training. *Journal of Applied Physiology*. 94(6): 2282-8.

175 Lüthi, J. M., Howald, H., Claassen, H., Rösler, K., Vock, P., & Hoppeler, H. (1986). Structural changes in skeletal muscle tissue with heavy-resistance exercise. *International Journal of Sports Medicine*, 7(03), 123-127.

most conclusive evidence shows that momentary fatigue using resistance stimulates the same growth of both types.[176]

All of which is to say, there's no point in worrying about your personal ratios of specific types of muscle fiber. You almost certainly don't know how much of each type you have, and it doesn't matter anyway. You can expect all your muscle fibers to grow and change in response to your activity, and strength training stimulates all types of muscle fiber quite effectively.

FALSEHOOD #7: TRAINING DIFFERENT RANGES OF MOTION

Some people believe you can grow muscle that works only in specific ranges of motion. In this theory, the range of motion trained becomes stronger while other ranges stay weaker. This is patently untrue. Let's use sprinters as an example. They use only seven degrees of action in their knee joints, yet they have 180 degrees available. If they were only getting stronger within those seven degrees of action, they'd be weak in all other ranges of motion and wouldn't even be able to get out of a chair. However, sprinters are strong in all ranges of motion.

Another common misconception is there are separate smaller muscles in the weak range of motion and bigger muscles in the strong range of motion. There is no scientific truth to this, and it doesn't even make sense from an anatomical perspective. When you contract a muscle, it changes length continuously during the contraction and covers some distance—but it's obviously the same muscle at any point during that process. Training any muscle increases its force production capacity and endurance.

---

176 Schoenfeld BJ. The mechanisms of muscle hypertrophy and their application to resistance training. (2010). *J Strength Cond Res.* Oct;24(10):2857-72.

This exercise benefit is applicable whenever you use that muscle, not in just some small portion of its contractile range.

You're exercising the same muscle at the bottom of the range as you are at the very top. By training that muscle in the strongest range of motion, you are increasing your strength far more overall than if you attempted to train at the bottom of the range where you are much weaker. Let's revisit the bench press research. It indicates people are unable to recruit as much of the muscle involved because nervous system activation of the muscle tissue is reduced at the bottom of the range of motion. This suggests the weak range of motion only limits the amount of weight you can train with even when the same muscles are involved. By training in the stronger range, you are able to trigger greater muscle growth.

John actually wrote a book about this subject called *Osteogenic Loading*. Here is an excerpt, with three peer-reviewed references:

> The strength in the myofibril development provided by this technology transfers to all ranges of motion. Because of the limited range of motion used in osteogenic loading, this brings up many questions. The simple answer is that, as the stimulus is engaged in the optimal biomechanical range of motion, by definition all-potential myofibrils are both involved, and stimulated. Therefore, even with low levels of myofibril involvement in the weaker ranges of motion, realize increases in strength. Barak, Ayalon, and Dvir (2004) demonstrated that limited range of motion resistance training is able to translate into full-range strength gains.[177] Johnston (2005) concluded, "no evidence exists to the effect that muscle

177 Barak, Y., Ayalon, M., & Dvir, Z. (2004). Transferability of strength gains from limited to full range of motion". *American College of Sports Medicine*. 36(8):1413-1420.

development is contingent on full range exercise."[178] Mookerjee, and Ratamess (1999) observed strength gains through the entire range of motion when isolating the optimal biomechanical position.[179] If this idea was true, sprinters would never be able to get out of a chair. They only use 7° out of 180° in knee bend. Anyone who says they are losing strength in the weak range, it's in their head or they're doing something else wrong.

Training only the weak range of motion leads to minimized training benefits in all ranges of motion. When researchers evaluated exercisers who intentionally engaged muscle during a weak range of motion during a bench press with conventional weights, they found "diminishing potentiation of the contractile elements during the upward movement together with the limited activity of the pectoral and deltoid muscles."[180] That is to say, the muscles driving the exercise motion were highly activated in the strong range, but were not well recruited by the nervous system in the weaker range. This suggests training the weak range of motion in isolation loads the same muscles but does not activate nearly as much of that muscle tissue.

The bottom line is, you can't train the ranges of motions separately. The mechanics and the muscle stimulated are the same no matter where you train.

---

178 Johnston, B (2005). The Effects of Fatigue from Limited Range Exercise on Full Range Function. *Journal of Exercise Physiology*. 8(5):15-21.

179 Mookerjee, S., & Ratamess N. (1999). Comparison of Strength Differences and Joint Action Durations Between Full and Partial Range-of-Motion Bench Press Exercise. *Journal of Strength and Conditioning Research*, 13(1), 76–81. National Strength & Conditioning Association.

180 Van Den Tillaar, R., & Ettema, G. (2010). The "sticking period" in a maximum bench press. *Journal of Sports Sciences*, 28(5), 529-535.

FALSEHOOD #8: ISOLATING PARTS OF A MUSCLE

This one is a variation on training the ranges of motion commonly espoused by bodybuilders. Here, people perform specific exercises in an attempt to change the shape of a specific muscle. Perhaps a bodybuilder wants their bicep to look more spherical in the center. In an attempt to change how it looks cosmetically, they decide to do hammer curls instead of regular ones.

This type of training regimen is ineffective due to basic physiological responses. You cannot change the distribution of the muscle tissue within the muscle unit to reshape it. As proof, studies show when your pectoral muscle contracts, the whole muscle contracts and not just a part of it.[181]

When people do incline presses to build their upper pectorals, all they're really doing is injuring their shoulder joints because the movement puts too much pressure there. Trying to isolate the upper pectoral in this way is probably responsible for the multitude of long-term bodybuilders who can barely lift their arms.

FALSEHOOD #9: THE ANABOLIC WINDOW

The concept behind the anabolic window is that there's a period of time right after a workout where the body is more apt to absorb protein and turn it into muscle. There is no scientific merit to this claim. The truth is, significantly elevated protein synthesis in response to exercise occurs for approximately thirty-six hours after training, a process that normally happens when you're sleeping.

---

181 Glass, S. C., & Armstrong, T. (1997). Electromyographical activity of the pectoralis muscle during incline and decline bench presses. *Journal of Strength and Conditioning Research*, 11, 163-167.

Given this statistic, it would be reasonable to assume the timing of eating following a workout makes no difference. However, the research here is somewhat murky. Several studies found protein consumption immediately following resistance training resulted in an improvement in hypertrophy—but the control group was not given the same supplemental protein as the test group. Therefore, the effect might be due to the increase in total daily protein rather than the specific timing of ingestion.[182,183] This conclusion is consistent with research discussed previously showing increased protein consumption leads to improved muscular growth, even when protein consumption is already very high compared to the recommendations of most standard dietary guidelines.

One study examining muscle hypertrophy in athletes specifically evaluated the effect of timing by comparing a test group consuming protein immediately before and after a workout to one consuming the same amount of protein at least five hours before and at least five hours after the workout. Experimenters concluded the "results indicate that the time of protein-supplement ingestion in resistance-trained athletes during a 10-wk training program does not provide any added benefit to strength, power, or body-composition changes."[184] Other research reports that while muscle protein synthesis following strength training may become unregulated by 50 percent at the four-hour mark, it actually accelerates and can be increased by more than 100 per-

---

182 Hulmi, J. J., Kovanen, V., Selänne, H., Kraemer, W. J., Häkkinen, K., & Mero, A. A. (2009). Acute and long-term effects of resistance exercise with or without protein ingestion on muscle hypertrophy and gene expression. *Amino Acids, 37*(2), 297-308.

183 Willoughby, D. S., Stout, J. R., & Wilborn, C. D. (2007). Effects of resistance training and protein plus amino acid supplementation on muscle anabolism, mass, and strength. *Amino Acids, 32*(4), 467-477.

184 Hoffman, J. R., Ratamess, N. A., Tranchina, C. P., Rashti, S. L., Kang, J., & Faigenbaum, A. D. (2009). Effect of protein-supplement timing on strength, power, and body-composition changes in resistance-trained men. *International journal of Sport Nutrition and Exercise Metabolism, 19*(2), 172-185.

cent twenty-four hours after the exercise session.[185] The results of this well-designed study, and the implications of the muscle protein synthesis timeline, strongly suggest that there is no need for an immediately post- or pre-workout meal.

Perhaps this idea arose out of bodybuilders who use carbohydrates to temporarily enlarge muscles. Bodybuilders often restrict carbs until right before a show, then eat several hundred grams post-workout. For instance, they might have a few Snickers bars. We once watched a bodybuilder eat three boxes of Fruity Pebbles. The carbs immediately go into the muscle in the form of glycogen, then convert to ATP (simplified explanation) and are held within the muscle. The muscles just blow up. They look huge.

Unfortunately, even with this type of timed eating, the effect is temporary. The muscle pump goes away. Muscles don't care about timing. They'll grow under the right conditions no matter when you choose to have a meal.

FALSEHOOD #10: TESTOSTERONE REPLACEMENT THERAPY (TRT) GIVES YOU AN ADVANTAGE

A lot of people think endocrinologist-prescribed TRT is an advantage. Essentially, they see TRT as a workaround to illegal steroids. Ask your doctor for it and they imagine you'll get the same types and quantities of anabolic chemicals cheating athletes might otherwise have to acquire illegally. They ask us how to get on TRT without even knowing if they need it, like it's a shortcut to achieving their body composition goals.

185 MacDougall, J. D., Gibala, M. J., Tarnopolsky, M. A., MacDonald, J. R., Interisano, S. A., & Yarasheski, K. E. (1995). The time course for elevated muscle protein synthesis following heavy resistance exercise. *Canadian Journal of Applied Physiology*, 20(4), 480-486.

We like to remind them that the "R" in TRT stands for replacement. Only people without enough naturally occurring testosterone are even eligible for TRT. When someone has low T, their doctor will only replace the amount of hormone that is supposed to be there under normal physiological conditions, not provide you the supernaturally high doses of testosterone used illegally by chemically "enhanced" athletes.

If you have high or normal testosterone, it wouldn't make sense to be on TRT anyhow. By definition, there would be no missing testosterone to replace, and in that case, it is unlikely any reputable physician would give it to you. What's more, if you start taking exogenous testosterone without having a deficiency, the medication could negatively impact normal testosterone production and cause serious cardiac problems. It's not worth it.

When correctly prescribed and used to resolve a naturally occurring deficiency, TRT certainly has its uses. John is on TRT because his testosterone tested at 163 nanograms to the deciliter when the normal range is between 270 and 1,020. His physician explained that without TRT, he'd be at risk of a heart attack because the testosterone receptors in the heart muscle are, in truth, more sensitive to testosterone than those in the skeletal muscle tissue, and thus the cells are heavily impacted by abnormally low levels of testosterone. So even though at the time John was in his thirties and playing semi-pro rugby, there was concern his cardiac muscle could be seriously compromised and put him at risk for serious complications without therapy. In light of this fact, his endocrinologist prescribed him with enough exogenous testosterone to bring him back to natural levels.

Our advice here is to have your levels tested if you think they might be low, but don't try to get on something you don't need. TRT is not an advantage or a shortcut for people with normal testosterone levels. Besides, you won't even be eligible if you're not at a deficit.

FALSEHOOD #11: USING CALORIC EXCESS TO STIMULATE MUSCLE

This theory holds that eating in an extreme caloric surplus will force muscle to grow, or make it grow faster. However, there's no force-feeding muscle. If you eat at a caloric surplus, you'll simply get fat because excess fat and carbohydrates get stored as body fat.

The only exception to this rule is if you're overfeeding with protein. In that case, the body can increase its metabolic rate to consume this protein, resulting in increased body temperature.[186] Called the thermogenic effect, this temperature increase happens because the body doesn't have a way to turn protein into fat. An interventional study performed in 2014 observed that weightlifters were able to maintain a hyper-caloric high-protein diet without gaining any body fat, which stands in stark contrast to older research showing that conventional hyper-caloric diets (in other words, overeating) led to weight gain.[187]

This myth has likely persisted because eating a lot of protein does help build muscle, so exercisers who ate massive amounts of food incidentally ended up eating upwards of one gram of

---

186 Johnston, C. S., Day, C. S., & Swan, P. D. (2002). Postprandial thermogenesis is increased 100% on a high-protein, low-fat diet versus a high-carbohydrate, low-fat diet in healthy, young women. *Journal of the American College of Nutrition*, 21(1), 55-61.

187 Antonio, J., Peacock, C. A., Ellerbroek, A., Fromhoff, B., & Silver, T. (2014). The effects of consuming a high protein diet (4.4 g/kg/d) on body composition in resistance-trained individuals. *Journal of the International Society of Sports Nutrition*, 11(1), 19.

protein per pound of body weight. That higher protein intake during the higher caloric intake led to more muscle growth than when consuming less food (and therefore, less protein). But these increased muscle gains were not a by-product of total calories, but rather eating the appropriate amount of protein.

In fact, a randomized, controlled trial showed eating very high levels of protein resulted in muscle gain even when maintaining a caloric deficit and experiencing significant fat loss. Those assigned a more moderate protein diet at the same level of caloric deficit did not build any muscle and experienced less fat loss.[188] This research strongly indicates the critical issue is protein consumption, and outside of increasing protein the only thing adding extra calories to your meal will do is make you fatter, not make more muscle faster.

FALSEHOOD #12: WIDE GRIP IS SUPERIOR

At strength competitions, competitors often take a wide stance for squats and deadlifts and a wider grip for bench pressing. While they might be able to lift more weight this way, that doesn't mean they're engaging more muscle tissue. Instead, they are shortening their range of motion and the lift and ultimately bypassing the strongest ranges of motion completely. The athletes don't care because, in a weightlifting competition, the bottleneck to success is the weak range.

This is fine for a contest, but not if your goal is to grow musculature. We kept the X3 bar at its current length to ensure users

188 Longland, T. M., Oikawa, S. Y., Mitchell, C. J., Devries, M. C., & Phillips, S. M. (2016). Higher compared with lower dietary protein during an energy deficit combined with intense exercise promotes greater lean mass gain and fat mass loss: a randomized trial. *The American Journal of Clinical Nutrition*, 103(3), 738-746.

take a narrow grip that maximizes muscle engagement. As John often says, "Wide grip is for your ego or a contest. Narrow grip is to grow."

FALSEHOOD #13: KETOGENESIS IS A NUTRITION PROGRAM

Many people think of ketogenesis as a diet or nutrition program, but it is actually a function of human physiology in which the body uses fat for fueling muscular contraction, organ function, and the general activities of daily living. We shift into a ketogenic state in the absence of glucose, such as when fasting. This process is typically well underway when going without food for eighteen hours or more.[189]

While a "keto diet" focuses on what nutritional choices you can make to maintain a ketogenic state even while continuously eating, this diet isn't necessary to get the benefits of ketogenesis. You simply need to be void of digestible calories to start using your own body fat as fuel. Someone could be eating a pure carbohydrate diet (although no one would recommend this) and still become ketogenic by fasting for eighteen-plus hours (check out the fasting section of this book in chapter 6 for more details on fasting).

Misinformation surrounding the ketogenic diet misled some people into believing they could eat all of the dietary fats they wanted while continuing to lose body fat. This obviously isn't true. And some people found out the hard way.

---

189 Anton, S. D., Moehl, K., Donahoo, W. T., Marosi, K., Lee, S. A., Mainous III, A. G., ...& Mattson, M. P. (2018). Flipping the metabolic switch: understanding and applying the health benefits of fasting. *Obesity*, 26(2), 254-268.

FALSEHOOD #14: CALORIE RESTRICTION IS THE BEST WAY TO LOSE BODY FAT

Although we touched on this concept in fasting and time-restricted eating, we wanted to clarify that research shows caloric restriction alone is not an effective fat loss method.

As we mentioned before, a key piece of research involved a Women's Health Initiative conducted randomized, controlled trial testing a low-fat, low-calorie approach to weight loss. This huge study of 50,000 women involved a 342-calorie average reduction of daily food intake and a 10 percent increase in exercise. The researchers projected a weight loss of thirty-two pounds over a SINGLE year based on basic thermodynamics arithmetic, but the actual results were much worse: despite good compliance, the test showed almost no weight loss (.04kg) over the course of seven years, not one single pound.[190]

A recent Type 2 diabetes study on younger people took a "calorie-deficit approach to decreasing energy intake by (specifically) limiting the intake of high fat, high sugar foods." At the beginning of the study, the BMI of the test subjects was thirty-four. After five years of calorie counting and deficits, the average BMI was still thirty-four. While some weight loss happened in the beginning of the study, subjects eventually put the weight back on EVEN WHILE STILL UNDER A DEFICIT. Why? Because their hormones changed to reach homeostasis.[191]

Research conducted as far back as 1957 provides further evidence that eating less does not necessarily create the need to

---

190 Howard, et al. (2006). Low-fat dietary pattern and weight change over 7 years: the Women's Health Initiative Dietary Modification Trial. *JAMA*. Jan 4;295(1):39-49.

191 TODAY Study Group. (2010). Design of a family-based lifestyle intervention for youth with type 2 diabetes: the TODAY study. *International Journal of Obesity (2005)*, *34*(2), 217.

burn body fat. Instead, it signals the body to slow down. Caloric reduction does not just selectively reduce adipose (body fat) deposits—wasting occurs with all body tissues, meaning muscle is lost along with fat. At the same time, hormones are driving appetite up. Being chronically undernourished is not what the body prefers, so as soon as calories go back up, even more fat is stored.[192]

Caloric restriction forces our metabolic rate to reach homeostasis, so ultimately—no matter how high the deficit—the body adjusts to it by using hormones and sacrificing muscle and other lean tissues to survive and maintain body fat. This is why we recommend fasting—no adjustment of this kind is needed. Extended fasts force the body to become leaner and preserve more muscle without calorie restriction.

WHERE THESE MYTHS ORIGINATED

Chances are you've tried one or more of these exercise fictions in your quest for health and fitness. You may even be upset at the suggestion they are untrue.

What may give you pause, however, is considering that the majority of recommendations most likely originated from someone who had simply succeeded in the gym—not a doctor, exercise scientist, physiologist, or, as is our case, a biomedical engineer. Myths like these often start because a regular person had success in the gym and attributed that success to a particular part of their routine, like specific movements, foods, or training regimens. That person told their lifting buddies, who told their friends, and so on. The legend lived on.

192 Thorpe, G. L. (1957). Treating overweight patients. *Journal of the American Medical Association*, 165(11), 1361-1365.

In some cases, like the anabolic window, the advice may even have worked—but not for the reasons people thought it did. For example, when drinking an extra protein shake right after a workout brought better results, people assumed the critical factor was the timing. Other people took the advice and benefitted, perpetuating the idea that timing was key, when actually the benefit came from the extra protein in their diet, regardless of timing. Eventually, entire gyms full of people were convinced they had to eat within a certain number of minutes after their workout, and they thought they had the results to prove it.

The particular habits of the most buff person at the gym probably aren't your most reliable source for exercise advice. Science is. Learning the truth, changing your habits, working out in a scientific manner is what will give you real, lasting results. And real, lasting results are not what most people achieve with the status quo.

CHAPTER 8

WHAT ABOUT GENETIC POTENTIAL?

In 1995, the Fat Free Mass Index (FFMI) study sought to determine an individual's genetic muscular potential. The research was unusual in that it included anabolic steroid users as examples of people who had gone beyond their genetic potential.

The analysis was rife with problems, the most blatant of which was researchers defined genetic potential based on inclusion criteria from an earlier study. This was, "we advertised in four gymnasiums in the Boston, Massachusetts, area and in three gymnasiums in the Santa Monica, California area to recruit subjects. We offered $60 for a confidential interview to any male aged 16 years or older who had lifted weights for at least 2 years."[193]

Think about two years of training at the age of sixteen. Is this when anyone reaches their genetic potential? Some people aren't

193 Pope, HG. Katz, DL. (1994). Psychiatric and Medical Effects of Anabolic-Androgenic Steroid Use: A Controlled Study of 160 Athletes. Arch Gen Psychiatry. 51(5):375–382.

even finished with puberty by then.[194] Also, consider the knowledge an average sixteen-year-old has. Do they train as optimally as a professional athlete? Do they get proper nutrition, or do they eat pizza and ice cream?

The FFMI was a disaster of a study, even from the author's standpoint. "Admittedly, one cannot definitively diagnose steroid use simply on the basis of the FFMI, much as one cannot make a definitive diagnosis of alcohol intoxication in a man who displays ataxia and dysarthria (slurring of words) upon getting out of his automobile."[195]

So can drug-tested athletes show us just how far our genetic potential can take us? Is the biggest difference in our genetics just how much anabolic hormones our bodies produce? The International Association of Athletics Federations recently made a decision on athletes with above normal testosterone as it applied to a particular female sprinter, Caster Semenya. She was barred from competition for having natural testosterone levels that are beyond what is considered normal for a female athlete.[196] So we know the position of the anti-doping agencies is that athletes need to be in a normal range.

If substantial hormonal variation is not allowed in drug-tested sports, but almost no athletes are affected by this rule (Semenya's case is extraordinarily unusual), then it would seem that

---

194 Kail, RV. Cavanaugh, JC. (2010). Human Development: A Lifespan View (5th ed.). *Cengage Learning*. p. 296.

195 Kouri, E. M., Pope, J. H., Katz, D. L., & Oliva, P. (1995). Fat-free mass index in users and nonusers of anabolic-androgenic steroids. Clinical journal of sport medicine: official *Journal of the Canadian Academy of Sport Medicine*, 5(4), 223-228.

196 Burns, K. (2019, May 15). Caster Semenya and the Twisted Politics of Testosterone. Retrieved from https://www.wired.com/story/caster-semenya-and-the-twisted-politics-of-testosterone/.

the hormonal playing field is fairly level. So who really has an advantage?

THE ACTUAL GENETIC DIFFERENCES BETWEEN ATHLETES AND REGULAR PEOPLE

We regularly see people on social media dismissing the success of an athletic individual as just "good genetics." This comment seems to be made most often by people lacking physical development. While it's unfortunate so many people have been misled in fitness, it's also easy to make excuses for failures or failed strategies. The reality is, there is no secret advantage you're missing.

NONSENSE FACTORS

"Everyone's taking performance-enhancing drugs" is an accusation we hear often. It's usually made by internet commenters who likely train using an inefficient standard program and eat the standard US 70 percent plant-based nutrition (which is really just crackers, noodles, and pizza) and are frustrated by their lack of results. Statistics show only 6.6 percent of men over the age of eighteen in the United States take or have taken steroids/performance-enhancing drugs.[197] And if only one percent of men are truly fit at all, that suggests at least six out of seven who use steroids and other drugs fail anyway. It's clearly not the difference in fit versus unfit people.

Low myostatin has been cited as a contributing factor in genetic potential. However, these observations were made in humans

---

197 W. E. Buckley, C. E. Yesalis, 3rd, K. E. Friedl, W. A. Anderson, A. L. Streit, J. E. Wright. JAMA. (1988) Estimated prevalence of anabolic steroid use among male high school seniors; 260(23): 3441-3445. Anabolic steroid use by male and female middle school students. *Pediatrics*. 101(5): E6.

with a rare myostatin mutation—you can count on one hand the people who have this worldwide. The only documented case of this mutation is in one child who has been under constant supervision for the sake of his cardiac health. His doctors are concerned that the excessive muscle mass could put too much of a strain on the cardiac system and end his life prematurely.[198]

REAL FACTORS

Higher birth weight is statistically associated with greater strength later in life.[199] Most likely, being born large and fed well as an infant contributes to becoming a bigger, stronger person as an adult. However, this finding does not take frame size into account. Being a taller or larger person with greater raw output doesn't necessarily equate to a higher power-to-weight ratio.

Strength athletes and NFL players often have a unique genetic layout of their tendons, giving them more power capability than normal people even in the weaker range.[200] As one study reports, "The location of a muscle's tendon insertion into bone is another factor contributing to maximal strength expression. The distance from the joint center to the point of tendon insertion represents the moment arm of muscle force, or the effort arm. A tendon inserted slightly further away from the joint poses a mechanical advantage for force production...a powerlifter would benefit more from a larger moment arm of force. Tendon

198 Schuelke, M., Wagner, K. R., Stolz, L. E., Hübner, C., Riebel, T., Kömen, W., ...& Lee, S. J. (2004). Myostatin mutation associated with gross muscle hypertrophy in a child. *New England Journal of Medicine, 350*(26), 2682-2688.

199 Barr, J. G., Veena, S. R., Kiran, K. N., Wills, A. K., Winder, N. R., Kehoe, S., ...& Krishnaveni, G. V. (2010). The relationship of birth weight, muscle size at birth and post-natal growth to grip strength in 9-year-old Indian children: findings from the Mysore Parthenon study. *Journal of Developmental Origins of Health and Disease*, 1(5), 329-337.

200 Sewell, D., Griffin, M., & Watkins, P. (2014). Sport and exercise science: An introduction. *Routledge.*

insertion is a genetic factor contributing to strength that does not change with training."[201] Another orthopedic study of this phenomenon states, "The tendon to bony insertion site varies dramatically along its length."[202]

The longer the lever arm is from the point of insertion, the more the mechanical advantage for the creation of force (seen via electromyography and force measurement), the more opportunity to activate muscle during movement. There is no way to change this; it is simply genetic.[203]

American football players are often seen as athletic strength athletes with diversity of skill—they can run fast and deliver force. The average NFL running back has a body weight of 232 pounds +/-18.7, and a percentage body fat of 16+/-4. The average NFL wide receiver has a body weight of 207.2 pounds +/-13.2, and a percentage body fat of 12.5+/-3.1.[204] These measures were taken via DEXA scans, which show ~4 percent higher than standard skin fold measurements.[205,206,207]

---

201 Ratamess, N. A. (2011). ACSM's foundations of strength training and conditioning. *Wolters Kluwer Health*/Lippincott Williams & Wilkins.

202 Thomopoulos, S., Williams, G. R., Gimbel, J. A., Favata, M., & Soslowsky, L. J. (2003). Variation of biomechanical, structural, and compositional properties along the tendon to bone insertion site. *Journal of Orthopaedic Research*, 21(3), 413-419.

203 Wilson, A., & Lichtwark, G. (2011). The anatomical arrangement of muscle and tendon enhances limb versatility and locomotor performance. Philosophical Transactions of the Royal Society B: Biological Sciences, 366(1570), 1540-1553.

204 Dengel, D. R., Raymond, C. J., & Bosch, T. A. (2017). Assessment of muscle mass. Body Composition: *Health and Performance in Exercise and Sport*. Boca Raton, FL: Taylor & Francis Group.

205 Kamp, P. (2019, November 13). Body Fat Percentage Distribution for Men and Women in the United States. Retrieved February 3, 2020.

206 Laurson, K. R., Eisenmann, J. C., & Welk, G. J. (2011). Body fat percentile curves for US children and adolescents. *American Journal of Preventive Medicine*, 41(4), S87-S92.

207 Borrud, L. G., Flegal, K. M., Freedman, D. S., Li, Y., & Ogden, C. L. (2011). Smoothed percentage body fat percentiles for US children and adolescents, 1999-2004.

What does this mean to X3 users? Because variable resistance off loads the weaker range of motion, the tendon factor becomes less relevant. This is also part of the reason for X3's custom banding. We wanted the highest level of variance in force possible, not only to address differences between weak and impact-ready ranges, but to also level the playing field for individuals who have "poor genetics" in terms of a less advantageous tendon layout.

CHAPTER 9

HYPERPLASIA

Arguably the most important questions in exercise physiology scientific research have always centered around understanding the mechanisms that can drive muscle adaptation to increase force production capacity, or more simply stated, ways for people to get stronger. The most accepted science dictates that muscles grow in size due to the growth of existing muscle fibers.

THE STRETCH EFFECT FOR EXTRA GROWTH

Some studies, however, have demonstrated that under extreme conditions of muscle size, lengthening, and workload, there is evidence that muscles can take advantage of an even more powerful mechanism. Muscle cells/fibers can split to form additional new fibers, a process called hyperplasia. Dr. Jose Antonio has been at the center of this controversial research and did his doctoral dissertation on the subject. The following covers his findings and supporting research, as well as a practical approach to using X3 to both trigger and amplify this effect to the maximum degree.

Hypertrophy refers to an increase in the size of the muscle cell/fiber while hyperplasia refers to an increase in the number of cells/fibers. Since this adaptation has been identified and confirmed, destruction of muscle cells/fibers has also been observed with endurance athletes when compared to individuals who have never trained for athletic adaptation in any way.[208,209]

When the body begins adapting to higher levels of force being put through a muscle, the adaptation is specific to help improve the tolerance of the imposed demand. So for example, the elements within a cell that aid in aerobic metabolism like mitochondria, do not increase in volume or performance with strength type exercise. Only the amount of contractile proteins is important in the context of maximum force production, and that is what grows. Single muscle cell/fiber hypertrophy does happen in two ways, sarcoplasmic and myofibrillar hypertrophy, but the instantaneous force production is only influenced by the amount of contractile proteins available, which is the myofibrillar effect.

Back in the 1970s, researchers began testing a stretching type stimulus with animals for extended periods in order to see how the muscle would adapt. While the parameters of this research made it impractical and unethical to perform with human test subjects, much was learned. For example, with a thirty-day stretching-type protocol, researchers observed a 172 percent increase in muscle mass and a 52–75 percent increase in muscle-

---

208 Costill, D. L., E. F. Coyle, W. F. Fink, G. R. Lesmes, and F. A. Witzmann. (1979). Adaptations in skeletal muscle following strength training. *J. Appl. Physiol.* 46(1): 96-99.

209 Tesch, P. A. and L. Larsson. (1982). Muscle hypertrophy in bodybuilders. *Eur. J. Appl. Physiol.* 49: 301-306.

fiber count.[210] This study was then replicated in 1991 with very similar results.[211]

CAN WE INDUCE THIS EFFECT IN HUMANS?

Throughout the natural growth progression from childhood to adolescence to adulthood, it has been shown that the continual passive mechanical stretch imposed by growing bone on muscle is responsible for muscular adaptations in length and size, including general mass adaptation.[212] Studies have been conducted that show that adolescents undergoing their growth spurt increase in lean body mass in a manner directly proportional to the growth of the skeleton.[213] This literature led to something called "bag theory."

Bag theory speaks to the constraints of the tissue that surrounds the muscle, called muscle fascia. Muscle does not exist in a vacuum, but rather it exists with a substantial connective tissue membrane surrounding it, which may be one of the major determinants of growth for that muscle. As referenced above, through natural growth, this connective tissue membrane stretches in humans, and muscle growth shortly follows. Also, proven through animal models, pressure applied to stretching of the muscle can facilitate growth. This argument is key in the "muscle memory" discussion. Since athletes who experience muscle mass loss through detraining can regain the

210 Sola, O. M., D. L. Christensen, and A. W. Martin. (1973). Hypertrophy and hyperplasia of adult chicken anterior latissimus dorsi muscles following stretch with and without denervation. *Exp. Neurol.* 41: 76-100.

211 Winchester, P. K., M. E. Davis, S. E. Alway, and W. J. Gonyea. (1991). Satellite cell activation of the stretch-enlarged anterior latissimus dorsi muscle of the adult quail. *Am. J. Physiol.* 260: C206-C212.

212 Gajdosik, R. L. 2001, "Passive extensibility of skeletal muscle: review of the literature with clinical implications," *Clin.Biomech.*(Bristol., Avon.), vol. 16, no. 2, pp. 87–101.

213 Millward, D. J. 1995, "A protein-stat mechanism for regulation of growth and maintenance of the lean body mass," *Nutr.Res.Rev.*, vol. 8, no. 1, pp. 93–120.

lost mass very easily, scientists have theorized that they benefit during retraining because the muscle fascia had previously been stretched or expanded and allowed a greater level of flexibility based on the extra mass that previously existed. This larger "container" for muscle tissue may then facilitate more rapid regrowth when the individual begins training again.

When looking at the physical mechanics of bag theory, the stretching of the fascia allows for more space inside of the muscle for hydration and for nutrients to be utilized by the muscle so that both sarcoplasmic and myofibril hypertrophy can be amplified. When this happens, another phenomenon has been shown to occur in the animal models of research. Hyperplasia occurs. So how do we know that hyperplasia can occur in humans just like in the animal models?

We know hyperplasia occurs in humans because of one particular study done with elite bodybuilders and powerlifters that had upper arm circumferences 27 percent greater than the normal non-exerciser control group yet the cross-sectional size of the athlete's muscle fibers in the triceps were not different than the controls, meaning there were more cells in the triceps.[214] Nygaard and Neilsen performed a similar study and showed similar results, so we know that humans can induce hyperplasia.[215] But based on what we have learned with the animal models, the biggest question is how do we create the largest stretch on the muscle without doing what was done to the ani-

---

214 Yamada, S., N. Buffinger, J. Dimario, and R. C. Strohman. (1989). Fibroblast growth factor is stored in fiber extracellular matrix and plays a role in regulating muscle hypertrophy. *Med. Sci. Sports Exerc.* 21(5): S173-S180.

215 Nygaard, E. and E. Nielsen. (1978). Skeletal muscle fiber capillarisation with extreme endurance training in man. *Swimming Medicine IV*(vol. 6, pp. 282-293). University Park Press, Baltimore.

mals, which was basically multi-day constant stretching of the muscle?

CREATING AN EXTENDED STRETCH EFFECT FOR EXTRA GROWTH

One of the problems with flexibility work via stretching singular muscles is that the extended flexibility of the target muscle is extremely temporary. A 2001 study took rapid measurements of flexibility adaptations after stretching sessions of specific muscles and determined that the effect begins to diminish after six minutes.[216] So how do we keep the effect of the stretch in place for extended periods of time? This is obviously needed for the more aggressive level of muscle protein synthesis and hyperplasia.

As you perform your X3 session, especially with the hypoxia-inducing constant tension technique, you will see a muscle blood flow increasing effect in the target muscle that is most likely beyond anything you have ever experienced. This effect can last for thirty minutes. So when an individual does a set, a thirty-second stretch of the target muscles will amplify this process and allow more blood flow into the muscle. Now, within (AND ONLY WITHIN) this thirty-minute window, you have the opportunity to do something that runs very contrary to almost everything else we say nutritionally. In that thirty-minute window, you could eat simple carbohydrates.

Don't let this confuse you. Carbohydrates play absolutely NO role in muscle protein synthesis and are not needed in any way to grow muscle, and more than ten studies have demonstrated

216 Spernoga, S. G., Uhl, T. L., Arnold, B. L., & Gansneder, B. M. (2001). Duration of maintained hamstring flexibility after a one-time, modified hold-relax stretching protocol. *Journal of Athletic Training*, *36*(1), 44.

this, including some that demonstrate that no organ in the body needs carbohydrates.[217,218,219,220,221,222,223,224,225,226,227] HOWEVER, carbohydrates play a role in the hydration of muscle cells and, not surprisingly, in the hydration of most other cells in the body. You retain two to three grams of water per gram of carbohy-

---

217 Staples AW, Burd NA, West DW, Currie KD, Atherton PJ, Moore DR, Rennie MJ, Macdonald MJ, Baker SK, Phillips SM. (2011). Carbohydrate does not augment exercise-induced protein accretion versus protein alone. *Med Sci Sports Exerc.*;43(7):1154–1161.

218 Koopman R, Beelen M, Stellingwerff T, Pennings B, Saris WH, Kies AK, Kuipers H, Van Loon LJ. (2007). Coingestion of carbohydrate with protein does not further augment postexercise muscle protein synthesis. *Am J Physiol Endocrinol Metab.*;293(3):E833–842.

219 Glynn EL, Fry CS, Timmerman KL, Drummond MJ, Volpi E, Rasmussen BB. (2013). Addition of carbohydrate or alanine to an essential amino acid mixture does not enhance human skeletal muscle protein anabolism. *J Nutr.*;143(3):307–314.

220 Hamer HM, Wall BT, Kiskini A, De Lange A, Groen BBL, Bakker JA, Gijsen AP, Verdijk LB, Van Loon LJC. (2013). Carbohydrate co-ingestion with protein does not further augment post-prandial muscle protein accretion in older men. *Nutr Metab*;10(1):15.

221 Cuthbertson D Smith K Babraj J et al. (2005). Anabolic signaling deficits underlie amino acid resistance of wasting, aging muscle. *FASEB Journal*;19:422–424.

222 Greenhaff, P. L., Karagounis, L. G., Peirce, N., Simpson, E. J., Hazell, M., Layfield, R., ...& Rennie, M. J. (2008). Disassociation between the effects of amino acids and insulin on signaling, ubiquitin ligases, and protein turnover in human muscle. *American Journal of Physiology-Endocrinology and Metabolism*, 295(3), E595-E604.

223 Volpi, E., Kobayashi, H., Sheffield-Moore, M., Mittendorfer, B., & Wolfe, R. R. (2003). Essential amino acids are primarily responsible for the amino acid stimulation of muscle protein anabolism in healthy elderly adults. *The American Journal of Clinical Nutrition*, 78(2), 250-258.

224 Moore, D. R., Churchward-Venne, T. A., Witard, O., Breen, L., Burd, N. A., Tipton, K. D., & Phillips, S. M. (2014). Protein ingestion to stimulate myofibrillar protein synthesis requires greater relative protein intakes in healthy older versus younger men. *Journals of Gerontology Series A: Biomedical Sciences and Medical Sciences*, *70*(1), 57-62.

225 Paddon-Jones, D., Campbell, W. W., Jacques, P. F., Kritchevsky, S. B., Moore, L. L., Rodriguez, N. R., & van Loon, L. J. (2015). Protein and healthy aging. *The American Journal of Clinical Nutrition*, *101*(6), 1339S-1345S.

226 US Food and Nutrition Board's 2005 textbook. Dietary Reference Intakes for Energy, Carbohydrate, Fiber, Fat, Fatty Acids, Cholesterol, Protein, and Amino Acids. 275-277.

227 Figueiredo, V. C., & Cameron-Smith, D. (2013). Is carbohydrate needed to further stimulate muscle protein synthesis/hypertrophy following resistance exercise? *Journal of the International Society of Sports Nutrition*, *10*(1), 42.

drates you intake.[228] This is part of the reason why so many suffer from high blood pressure. They are constantly overconsuming carbohydrates and driving their blood pressure up because of water retention. However, in our case, we first deplete muscle glycogen, then replenish it immediately using carbohydrates, and after stretching the entire muscle and creating more room within the cells and within the entire muscle fascia, we create a hyper-hydration environment which enables accelerated muscle protein synthesis.

In 2004, one of the most important studies to support the hypothesis of muscle fascia stretching delivering better cellular hydration and accelerated muscle growth was published. This study concluded, "Thus the pressurization of L6 cells (mammal skeletal muscle) stimulated lactate utilization and glucose uptake. These findings suggest that mechanical pressure enhanced aerobic metabolism in skeletal muscle cells and may provide valuable clues toward elucidating the nervous system-independent mechanism(s) for metabolic activation and/or adaptation by skeletal muscle contraction." This means that by increasing the pressures within the cell, more muscle growth can occur.[229]

It seems 2004 was a popular year for research around the immediate post-workout replenishment of glycogen in musculature, because another case study came out then. This one concluded, "For rapid recovery from prolonged exercise, it is important

228 Steen, J. (2017, November 6). We Found Out If Carbs Really Make You Look 'Puffy' And Retain Water. Retrieved March 7, 2020, from https://www.huffingtonpost.com.au/2017/11/05/do-carbs-make-you-retain-water_a_23265193/#:~:text=%22Carbohydrate%20intake%20can%20lead%20to,in%20providing%20energy%20between%20meals.

229 Morita, N., Iizuka, K., Okita, K., Oikawa, T., Yonezawa, K., Nagai, T., ... & Kawaguchi, H. (2004). Exposure to pressure stimulus enhances succinate dehydrogenase activity in L6 myoblasts. *American Journal of Physiology-Endocrinology and Metabolism*, 287(6), E1064-E1069.

to replenish muscle glycogen stores and initiate muscle tissue repair and adaptation…To maximize muscle glycogen replenishment, it is important to consume a carbohydrate supplement as soon after exercise as possible."[230] Low and researchers demonstrated earlier that this environment could better transport amino acids to facilitate greater muscle protein synthesis, concluding "Hyper-hydration also may have a direct effect on amino acid transport systems."[231] Most recently in 2014 another study has confirmed these same findings, concluding: "Cellular swelling, often referred to as "the pump," has been shown to mediate increase in muscle protein synthesis and decrease protein degradation."[232]

WHAT IS THE BEST PROTOCOL FOR HYPER-HYDRATION OF MUSCLE?

Now, this may just sound like the opportunity to have an incredible "cheat meal." Not the case. In fact, a relatively small amount of carbohydrates are required to replenish muscle glycogen even in a stretched muscle. Consuming 0.5–0.7 grams of carbs per pound (1.1–1.5 grams/kg) of body weight within thirty minutes after training results in proper glycogen resynthesis.[233,234] So

230 Ivy, J. L. (2004). Regulation of muscle glycogen repletion, muscle protein synthesis and repair following exercise. *Journal of Sports Science & Medicine, 3*(3), 131.

231 Low SY, Rennie MJ, and Taylor PM. (1997). Signaling elements involved in amino acid transport responses to altered muscle cell volume. *FA SEB J* 11: 1111–1117.

232 Schoenfeld, B. J., & Contreras, B. (2014). The muscle pump: potential mechanisms and applications for enhancing hypertrophic adaptations. *Strength & Conditioning Journal, 36*(3), 21-25.

233 Kerksick, C. M., Arent, S., Schoenfeld, B. J., Stout, J. R., Campbell, B., Wilborn, C. D., …& Willoughby, D. (2017). International society of sports nutrition position stand: nutrient timing. *Journal of the International Society of Sports Nutrition, 14*(1), 33.

234 Haff, G. G., Koch, A. J., Potteiger, J. A., Kuphal, K. E., Magee, L. M., Green, S. B., & Jakicic, J. J. (2000). Carbohydrate supplementation attenuates muscle glycogen loss during acute bouts of resistance exercise. *International Journal of Sport Nutrition and Exercise Metabolism, 10*(3), 326-339.

for a 200-pound male lifter for example, this would, on the higher side, be 140g of carbohydrates. That would be approximately three cups of rice. White rice absorbs rather quickly, therefore it is a good choice for this endeavor. There is insulin secretion with this process, but it's lower than if there was no workout because the insulin and glucose should be matched, thus absorbing into muscle quickly. This keeps users of this practice from having the sugar cravings normally associated with carbohydrate intake.

Amplification of this process can come from vasodilation or other methods of encouraging extracellular hydration. There are four possibilities that we are aware of:

- **Creatine monohydrate.** Our least favorite cellular hydration amplifier. Creatine occurs naturally in animal proteins and has no side effects, but in its isolated form, it has been seen to exacerbate bipolar disorder, kidney dysfunctions, and Parkinson's disease. It has also been extensively tested as a weightlifting supplement, with unimpressive results.
- **Glycerol.** Once on the banned substance list for some strange reason, this supplement will attract water and in effect increase blood flow into muscle with a vasodilatory (opening of blood vessels) effect. If you choose this option, use the Hydromax versions. The straight glycerol powder will likely give you diarrhea and compromise digestion of all nutrients you consume later that day.
- **Epimedium.** This is a vasodilation agent that will increase blood flow all over the body. Many fake Viagra-type products are made of this, as it has a similar, albeit far weaker, effect.
- **Viagra/Levitra/Cialis (prescription vasodilator).** Probably the most powerful way to amplify muscular cellular hydra-

tion beyond carbohydrate consumption alone. Obviously, you would need a prescription for these medications. We do not advise walking into your physician's office and talking about a prescription vasodilator for the purposes of muscle building. Many physicians would not understand this as a need and will deny you the prescription. You may consider going down this path if you have other legitimate reasons for qualifying for the prescription, as determined by you and your physician. This has been specifically demonstrated in clinical literature to increase the amount of muscle protein synthesis.[235]

Steps to amplified growth and hyperplasia are as follows:

1. Approximately one hour before your workout time, you will take whatever it is you decided to amplify cellular hydration and blood flow, meaning creatine/glycerol/epimedium/prescription vasodilator.
2. Do your normal workout, assuming X3, and keep constant tension so that your hypoxia and blood flow are at their absolute maximum and never do less than fifteen reps. The "pump" from this workout will be one of the largest you have ever felt.
3. After the workout, stretch all the target muscles for thirty seconds each. We aren't going to recommend any particular types of stretch for individual muscles because throughout life we all have slight joint pain and dysfunctions (this is an example of where many people are different). We want you to pick the stretches that feel the most comfortable. This takes the already present "pump" extra blood flow and

---

235 Sheffield-Moore, M., Wiktorowicz, J. E., Soman, K. V., Danesi, C. P., Kinsky, M. P., Dillon, E. L., ...& Lynch, J. P. (2013). Sildenafil increases muscle protein synthesis and reduces muscle fatigue. *Clinical and Translational Science*, *6*(6), 463-468.

amplifies it based on the fascia stretching described earlier. So here the stretch and the extra blood flow are working together in a synergistic manner.

4. As soon as possible, and definitely before thirty minutes have passed since the end of your workout, consume between 0.5–0.7 grams of carbs per pound (1.1–1.5 grams/kg) of body weight. This replenishes the spent glycogen stores and can amplify the stretch effect within the muscle to increase muscle protein synthesis and trigger hyperplasia.
5. (Optional for those doing fasting) Eat your one meal for the day, or enter your eating window, where you may have two meals. You want to make sure that when your appetite is stimulated from the carbohydrates, you take advantage of that fact and get as much high-quality protein as possible. As stated earlier, one gram per pound of body weight, or 2.2g/kg of body weight.

CHAPTER 10

JOHN'S PROTOCOL

Before X3, I used to believe I had terrible genetics for activating muscle. I'd been doing standard lifting and consuming a gram of protein per pound of body weight (2.2 g per kg of body weight) per day for twenty years—plus I had a prescription for testosterone replacement therapy (TRT)—and I'd only managed to put on body fat without experiencing much change in my strength or size. Once I started using X3, my body composition totally transformed and now I have the same kind of stats as an NFL player.

JOHN'S NUTRITION AND TYPICAL TRAINING HABITS

There are quite a few people who have seen results equal to or better than mine in terms of building mass, continuing to stay lean, and losing body fat with X3. Some have gained twenty or more pounds of lean muscle in six months or less—even faster than I did. But because I was the first to use X3, conducted all the research behind it, and have certainly had a time-of-use advantage, I still receive many questions about my personal X3 and nutrition protocol.

This admittedly has not always fully matched my recommendations for typical users. For example, I'd been in a mild state of ketogenesis for almost ten years before inventing X3. When I started testing the prototype, I decided to delve further into nutritional research to determine the recommendations that would ensure the greatest user success. This led to a growing knowledge around protein needs for muscle protein synthesis and time-restricted eating/fasting for decreased body fat and muscle maintenance.

I ended up combining these two elements—fasting and high protein—into my diet. I soon found there wasn't much room left in the intestines for anything but the animal protein I was eating to meet my protein goals during my one giant meal a day. Thinking a strictly carnivore diet was too crazy for most people to adopt at the time, I recommended a standard, easy-to-follow ketogenic diet instead.

I did, however, come clean that I was doing something a little more serious: a near zero carbohydrate, all protein, one meal a day (OMAD) plan. Not formally recommending my way of eating but just posing it as an idea seemed to make it more appealing to other people. Many ended up giving it a shot and got fantastic results as well.

A few months after I started eating this way, I met Dr. Shawn Baker, one of my favorite people. He had just been on *The Joe Rogan Experience* podcast talking about carnivore nutrition, and I realized then maybe my plan wasn't so unreasonable to recommend after all. Baker had tens of thousands of users in his carnivore group on Facebook who'd experienced incredible fat loss results as well as reductions in chronic diseases (some of which had previously been associated with meat consumption in highly biased studies). After speaking with Dr. Baker and being on his podcast, I became much more comfortable giving the general recommendation of high amounts of animal protein—mostly because people need to hit their protein minimums, but also because the body uses animal protein more efficiently than vegetable sources.

THE FIRST TWO YEARS

I gained thirty pounds of muscle mass in the first year of using X3, then fifteen more in the second year. During this period of time, I also lost sixteen pounds of body fat. At the time there were no supplements I felt were worth taking, so I wasn't bothering with any of that. I was just doing the standard X3 sessions, six days per week.

On a normal day, I'd start with a bulletproof coffee—black coffee with a teaspoon of butter and medium-chain triglycerides (MCT) oil blended in. Because I flew a few hundred thousand miles a year to attend medical conferences as well as clinic openings with my first invention, OsteoStrong, this became a difficult habit to maintain. Traveling with grass-fed butter and MCT oil was a real pain. Even with ice packs, the butter would get soft and seep into the edges of the container so when I opened it, there was a mess. Same for the MCT oil: it is very thin and also tended to leak out of its container, especially under altitude pressure. I eventually started drinking plain black coffee instead, which led to me deciding to develop my own natural coffee replacement beverage, which eventually became another Jaquish Biomedical product In-Perium. It's a great appetite suppressant that kept me from being too hungry on OMAD.

My one meal was typically two or three large steaks. My body weight was approaching 220 pounds, so I needed to be at or over 220 grams of high-quality protein to meet my protein needs. As I experimented with forty-eight- and seventy-two-hour fasted periods, I discovered you can really be as lean as you want while maintaining muscle mass if you are willing to put up with multiple days of zero food at all.

PROTOCOLS IN THE THIRD YEAR

My success led me to take a more aggressive approach in the third year, which brings us to the present.

Since the development of Fortagen, I and several other X3 users have demonstrated taking three to five doses daily builds muscle on an almost zero-calorie day (Fortagen is four calories per dose). It doesn't break the autophagic cell recycling process since more than fifty calories are required to do that.[236]

Fortagen was designed to help individuals who want to eat less animal protein or just find it difficult, inconvenient, or expensive to eat multiple pounds/kilograms of meats on a daily basis to meet their protein needs. It has been an incredible tool for staying at a caloric maintenance number while still getting an excess of quality protein. Fortagen helps me continue to build muscle and maintain a fasted state at the same time.

So when and how long do I fast these days? If I am above 10 percent body fat as measured by whatever test I'm utilizing—which is typically DEXA or the Department of Defense circumference measurement test—I go five days eating only sixteen calories

236 Glynn, E. L., Fry, C. S., Drummond, M. J., Timmerman, K. L., Dhanani, S., Volpi, E., & Rasmussen, B. B. (2010). Excess leucine intake enhances muscle anabolic signaling but not net protein anabolism in young men and women. *The Journal of Nutrition*, 140(11), 1970-1976.

of Fortagen per day. When I start eating normally again, I've typically dropped a few pounds of body fat and gained a few of muscle. This is only viewable after the rehydration, which can take a few days.

When I am below 10 percent body fat, and preferably below 8 percent, I stick to leaner cuts of meat, get at least 150 grams of protein from the meats I eat, and take one dose of Fortagen in the morning and another one thirty minutes before bed. This pattern keeps me perpetually growing muscle while still maintaining a very lean physique. Of course, if I have a photo shoot, I may cut water out for twenty-four hours beforehand so I look even leaner. For example:

As I mentioned before, Jaquish Biomedical Corporation now has a coffee replacement product that can also be used pre-workout. In-Perium has a number of ingredients like electrolytes to keep you hydrated, suppress appetite, and help maintain a fasted state. I only use this as a coffee replacement, however, since I don't drink coffee pre-workout.

Caffeine is a vasoconstrictor, meaning it slightly restricts blood flow and stimulates an increased heart rate and blood pressure. It's a great way to start the day, but not my favorite pre-workout protocol because there are benefits to doing the exact opposite—vasodilating. Since cellular hydration is associated with increased levels of muscle protein synthesis,[237] I try to vasodilate through a combination of stretching a muscle, then hydrating that muscle to the highest degree immediately post workout. The strategy has accelerated my growth and I intend to continue it.

From a training perspective, my workouts haven't changed since day one. My emphasis has always been on doing slow and controlled movements. Two seconds up and two seconds down is the cadence that encourages stability firing for growth hormone upregulation as well as a greater level of fatigue. The main objective is not to "do reps," but to get to the absolute maximum level of exhaustion so the central nervous system initiates anabolic hormones and growth factors to build muscular tissue at the fastest rate possible.

---

237 Ivy, J. L. (2004). Regulation of muscle glycogen repletion, muscle protein synthesis and repair following exercise. *Journal of Sports Science & Medicine*, 3(3), 131.

CONCLUSION

After reading all this research, a handful of people might still feel inclined to argue that the fitness industry benefits are "tried and true," having worked well for decades. But really, that couldn't be farther from the truth. If you're still inclined to hold on to convention, please consider our argument about the status quo.

THE FITNESS INDUSTRY HAS A 99 PERCENT FAILURE RATE

"Programs should be judged based on results, not intentions."

—MILTON FRIEDMAN, ECONOMIST, NOBEL PRIZE WINNER

We have been told, "time is money." Therefore, investing your time should be viewed as at least as important as investing your money. Now, when it comes to the concept of investment, would you ever invest your money with a money-management company that lost 99 percent of its clients' funds? Of course, you wouldn't. No one would. Yet millions invest their time in the fitness industry. How good of an investment is this? Let us take a critical look at the industry and its results.

What metrics do we look at when judging how the fitness industry performs? The industry itself and its trade publications frequently reference fitness membership sales and home-equipment sales. But is this success of the customer? No, it isn't. Success of the customer should be judged by actually getting in athletic condition.

So what percentage of the population actually achieves this? The fitness industry will not tell you—because they don't pay for it to be analyzed, most likely because they don't want you to know the answer. We did however find a financial analysis group who compiled this data and published the bleak results.

PARAMETERS OF ANALYSIS

The Centers for Disease Control and Prevention (CDC) has the responsibility of producing vital and health statistics for the nation. They fund an annual project to collect health, fitness, and nutritional data from a broad population, designed to reflect the general population. Called the National Health and Nutritional Examination Survey (NHANES), it interviews 5,000 people per year in the United States based on metrics of nutrition, exercise habits, general health, and disease states.[238]

The industry fails to attract the majority of the population, but maybe the reasons for this are based on the casual observations of the uninvolved. Maybe they see those who engage in exercise and fail to observe physiological changes. If the average person who has never exercised has five friends that do, this individual may ask themselves, "What results are my friends getting?" If

238 NHANES 2015-2016 Overview. (2018, October 30). Retrieved February 3, 2020, from https://wwwn.cdc.gov/nchs/nhanes/continuousnhanes/overview.aspx?BeginYear=2015.

the answer to this question is "No results or hardly any results," this is a poor motivator for that casual observer.

It turns out the most recent set of data on the subject states, "21.9% of men and 17.5% of women were strength training 2 or more times per week in 2004."[239] As we are looking at body composition, we decided to focus this analysis on strength training, as opposed to cardio. As you learned in the hormonal section, cardiovascular exercise has a tendency of making body composition worse, not better, due to muscle loss from cortisol upregulation.

In order to get a more accurate success versus failure rate in the industry, we determined only looking at males would be more useful. Females can have different goals from one another, some wanting just to reshape one body part, for example, so they just do one exercise, whereas males tend to have the similar goal of improved body composition.

Percentage of body fat/body composition is the preferred metric, because it takes both an individual's muscularity and fat mass into consideration. Meaning, as people add muscular mass while not also adding fat mass, they are lowering their body fat percentage.

So who are the males with the best body composition? The top one percentile of low body fat adult males in the US is at 10.6 percent, based on a four-year analysis of the NHANES

239 Chevan, J. (2008). Demographic determinants of participation in strength training activities among US adults. *The Journal of Strength & Conditioning Research*, 22(2), 553-558.

database, N= 20,000.[240] This is a body fat percentage level that would be on the bottom end of what most people would call "athletic looking." Even the average of the top 1 percent is not so impressive (note: NFL players' body fat is mentioned elsewhere in this book, but that sport rewards people for being heavier, so for this particular comparison, we exclude them).

For the sake of the argument, however, let's call these people "fit." Essentially, the 20.9 percent of the population who engage in regular strength training fail to reach the body fat levels required to appear "fit." And 78.1 percent of the population won't be bothered to engage in such activity. And why would they? Just by observation, the effort seems futile.

DON'T STEROIDS DISTORT EVERYONE'S VISION OF WHAT "FIT" REALLY IS?

"Everyone who is bigger than me is on steroids. Everyone who is smaller than me doesn't train hard."

—TESTOSTERONE NATION, QUOTING INTERNET COMMENTERS

Jealous people are masterful with excuses to cover their own eyes from potential self-blame (taking responsibility). But still, let's explore what performance-enhancing drugs have done for the general population so we can make sure this variable has not skewed general public opinion of what is possible.

So 6.6 percent of males over eighteen have used or are using anabolic steroids in the United States.[241] Consider this statistic along

240 Kamp, P. (2019, November 13). Body Fat Percentage Distribution for Men and Women in the United States. Retrieved February 3, 2020, from https://dqydj.com/body-fat-percentage-distribution-men-women/.

241 W. E. Buckley, C. E. Yesalis, 3rd, K. E. Friedl, W. A. Anderson, A. L. Streit, J. E. Wright. (1988) Estimated prevalence of anabolic steroid use among male high school seniors; 260(23): 3441-3445. Anabolic steroid use by male and female middle school students. *Pediatrics*. 101(5): E6.

with the data presented above. One percent of the population is borderline fit, and 6.6 percent have used anabolic drugs. Even if all of the fit people were anabolic drug users (and clearly not all of them are), this means roughly six out of seven people who use anabolic drugs still fail to achieve a relevant level of conditioning despite the "advantage" they have. So are these anabolic steroids the gateway to perfect conditioning? Obviously not.

There are two reasons almost the entire population fails to see any results from standard fitness. These are stimulus and nutrition. Nutrition, of course, doesn't matter if the stimulus isn't effective. Therefore primarily, the stimulus for growth—meaning existing training protocols—does not stimulate much growth at all. While traditional resistance training has been demonstrated to positively affect muscle hypertrophy, the loads required to increase myofibril hypertrophy are difficult if not impossible to achieve with current technology. Petrella, (2008), in the *Journal of American Physiology* analyzed myofibril development in a test group and made the observation that, out of sixty-six subjects they selected, seventeen had either no or nominal myofibril response to a conventional resistance training protocol.[242] Intensity of stimulus is directly related to adaptive responses in the human body. Make sure you understand this because it means that 25.7 percent of people who engaged in strength training were unable to stimulate muscle-protein synthesis.

WHERE FITNESS FAILED

As we're fond of saying, and just outlined in detail above, fitness may well be humanity's most failed endeavor. Almost every other sector has shown vast improvement over the past fifty

242 Petrella, J. K., Kim, J. S., Mayhew, D. L., Cross, J. M., & Bamman, M. M. (2008). Potent myofiber hypertrophy during resistance training in humans is associated with satellite cell-mediated myonuclear addition: a cluster analysis. *Journal of Applied Physiology*, 104(6), 1736-1742.

or so years, with computers and cars being prime examples. If you're driving a newer car, your odds of dying in a car accident are reduced by a huge margin compared to a decade ago. If you go back ten more years, that reduction is even more marked. Similarly, computers took up an entire room back in the 1970s, while today we carry far more powerful computers in our pockets in the form of smartphones. Innovation has been fast and furious.

But as for the fitness industry? It hasn't seen any improvements since the 1950s or '60s. Consider the fitness franchise Curves. Designed to be a quick and efficient strength training circuit for busy women, it didn't innovate in any particular way other than creating a social exercise environment. It was a fad. Where Curves were once ubiquitous, now the franchise is hugely contracted and no longer relevant.

All of which is to say, there always seems to be a new flavor of exercise being touted as the holy grail of fitness—right now, treadmill and cycling studios are having a heyday—yet nothing they teach us is ever fundamentally different than practices dating back half a century or more. The first patent for a device recognizable as a treadmill was granted in 1913 and "treadwheels" existed as early as Ancient Rome, although there was no concept of aerobic exercise back then, so it was simply a method of transmitting mechanical power. The first invention approximating a stationary bike dates back to 1796 (it was called the Gymnasticon). Bringing group video workouts to these machines is certainly new, modern, and trendy, but the underlying exercise methodology is very, very old and not likely to suddenly start generating great outcomes beyond what we have seen before. And most people are not achieving great results. It's all the same thing, different year.

While reading this book, you have no doubt noticed the peer-reviewed journal *Medicine & Science in Sports & Exercise* regularly referenced. This is one of five journals the American College of Sports Medicine (ACSM) publishes on a regular basis. Despite the ACSM being one of the most impressive and thorough educational and research bodies in the field of sports science, they have a tremendous problem: personal trainers and the fitness industry in general do not seem to know much about this organization.

What's worse is much of the scientific discovery documented by the ACSM never seems to make it into the fitness industry's instruction to its customers. This is why personal trainers continue to teach so many previously disproven principles of exercise physiology. Perhaps the certifying bodies for the exercise training industry are just not updating their curriculum, or maybe individuals involved in the industry treat it as a temporary job and are not really making it a career. Maybe it's because trainers aren't paid very well, mostly because many consumers would be priced out of using them if rates were higher. No matter the reason, the fact remains that much of what instructors teach gym goers has been disproven or is a misunderstanding of real principles.

FILLING IN THE GAPS WITH SCIENCE

A recent poll conducted in the United Kingdom showed a mere 3 percent of women are happy with the way their body looks. Some blame photoshopped advertisements, others look to social media as the culprit. However, these things are not changing anytime soon.

In reality, people are in worse shape than ever. Obesity and Type 2 diabetes are full-on epidemics. If current common knowledge about fitness was effective, these problems wouldn't be widespread. They would have been long eradicated.

It seems the truth about the best way to get results through exercise had simply not been disseminated effectively before this book. Although well-documented, well-researched, peer-reviewed literature exists, the general public has remained in the dark about it. And certainly, no means of translating this research into a practical workout method existed until now.

When we discovered the gaping hole that existed between the scientifically proven methods of achieving health and fitness and the methods comprising "conventional wisdom," we knew we had to take action. Through exhaustive research, we were able to develop X3, the at-home, time-efficient fitness solution for optimizing lean tissue and muscle mass, as well as Fortagen, the most anabolic-efficient protein supplement available. With these, we believe we've solved the inherent problems that continue to exist in the fitness field today.

A MIND IS LIKE A PARACHUTE—IT DOESN'T WORK UNLESS IT'S OPEN

Many people are emotionally committed to inefficient exercise programs because that's what they've been taught and always done. As a result, they get mad when we inform them what they "know" about fitness is most likely wrong. But if you're not getting the results you're seeking from your exercise routine—especially after years of working out—why not try something science has shown is the better, more effective way to meet your goals?

We understand that what we're saying in this book might sound radical, since we're dismissing concepts that are widely accepted as fact. You might even be wondering how what we're saying can be true, since so many people believe otherwise. But given how well fitness is working out for most people—which is to say, not well at all—perhaps you'll begin to see that the field is full of mistaken ideas and concepts.

PUTTING KNOWLEDGE INTO ACTION

An industry, or ANY industry, with a 99 percent failure rate, such as this, should be ignored in favor of an alternative approach. Here, we have offered one. Now it's up to you to put your newfound knowledge to use.

Most people are still searching for the best way to significantly improve their body composition, muscularity, and health. Unfortunately, much of what we've been taught about fitness simply has no scientific backing—which is probably why the majority of us haven't come close to achieving our fitness goals yet. As the saying goes, "Doing the same thing over and over and expecting different results is the definition of insanity."

After reading this book, though, you know better. You know the most effective, efficient way to activate your muscles and stimulate hormone release. You know how to eat for optimal results. And you know why your efforts may not have achieved your desired outcomes before.

You now have the knowledge and tools you need to become the healthiest, leanest, most muscular version of yourself you can be. All you have to do is apply everything you've learned here. Stay consistent and disciplined and your results will astound you. We have faith in you!

APPENDIX

THE PROTOCOL

Now that we've discussed our scientific conclusions regarding exercise, nutrition, the science of health in general—which in no small part has consisted of us pointing out the many things in fitness that are *not* effective—as well as describing the development of our X3 product, you may be wondering: what do we recommend you actually do?

Work out with X3, of course. The X3 protocol is straightforward and easy to follow. There are four exercises per workout, each performed to full exhaustion far beyond what you can get from weights. Beginning users exercise four days a week and then progress to a six-day- per-week routine.

BAND OPTIONS

There are four bands included with the X3 system. These fit the needs of most users in terms of resistance throughout the range of motion. For a small percentage of people who need more force, there's an additional extra-heavy band, called the Elite Band, available as an accessory.

BAND COLOR	EXERCISES AND RESISTANCE	
	SINGLE	**DOUBLED**
	Squats, Overhead Presses, Bicep Curls, Upright Row (optional)	Chest Presses, Tricep Presses, Pec Crossovers, Deadlifts, Bent Rows, Calf Raises
White	10 to 50 pounds	Up to 100 pounds
Light Grey	25 to 80 pounds	Up to 160 pounds
Dark Grey	50 to 110 pounds	Up to 220 pounds
Black	60 to 140 pounds	Up to 280 pounds
Elite	110 to 310 pounds	Up to 620 pounds

The force numbers listed above are based on testing with a typical six-foot-tall user. Resistance provided may be slightly more or less depending on your height and the relative length of your arms, legs, and torso.

Although this is not usually an issue, there's a subset of the population for whom the included four bands are initially too heavy. If someone finds they need a lighter band—for example, to do the overhead press, which for many people is the most difficult exercise—we advise selecting one of the many ultralight bands available from other companies.

CHOOSING A BAND

In the interest of safety, we recommend starting with the lightest band. The goal for each exercise is to do as many slow and controlled full repetitions as possible, followed by partial repetitions until exhaustion. The cadence of these repetitions should be four seconds per repetition, meaning two seconds up and two seconds down.

If you can complete more than forty full repetitions with the lightest band, you should select a band with higher resistance for that particular exercise the next time you are scheduled to do it. Continue this process until you find a band that allows you to do at least fifteen repetitions but not forty. Stay with that band until you become strong enough to move up yet again.

Be sure to pick a weight you can handle and control through the entire range of motion. We don't want you dropping the bar and injuring yourself. Rest assured you'll still get superior stimulus because you're handling more force in the stronger range of motion—which cannot be said of standard iron weight.

Fifteen repetitions are the minimum you should be able to complete. If you cannot complete this number, the band is too heavy and for safety reasons you should go lighter. Some people who have been weightlifting for a long time feel fifteen is a high repetition count. However, X3 uses more weight and delivers it throughout all ranges of motion, so it can't be compared to regular weightlifting. Strength curves show maximum capabilities in different positions of a movement are not linear.

REPETITIONS

The X3 protocol calls for fifteen to forty repetitions for each of the four exercises included in that day's workout. Be sure to maintain constant tension on the bands as you perform each repetition. This means not EVER letting there be slack in the band at the bottom, and not EVER locking out at the top of a movement. This ensures the muscle never relaxes, and induces the hypoxic effect described in earlier chapters. (See the infographic later in this chapter for a closer look at constant tension.)

The aim is to go to exhaustion. Once you can no longer complete full repetitions, continue doing half and quarter repetitions. In this way, you're exhausting all ranges of motion.

For instance, you might complete thirty full repetitions. Then you may achieve ten half repetitions and five quarter repetitions before becoming unable to continue any further.

WORKING TO EXHAUSTION

With X3, the goal is to continue each exercise until you can no longer move the bar. The last repetition should barely move it an inch.

Working out with X3 brings a deeper level of exhaustion than expected with weight training. You'll go from full repetitions to partial repetitions until you reach something akin to mechanical failure. When the partial repetitions slow to almost nothing, only then is it time to quit. The biggest benefit comes from your last repetitions, not the first ones. We call this "Diminishing Range." This is very important to the protocol.

In between exercises, take the time you need to catch your breath and recover cardiovascularly. The exact timing is personal, and a more muscular person will take longer to recover because more blood is flowing through them. In most cases, recovery only takes a minute or so.

WORKOUT FREQUENCY

X3 is a tough workout, and it will take several weeks for your body to adjust to it. Starting with a lighter workout schedule will help during this adjustment period. Therefore, if you are new to lifting and not already a serious athlete, we recommend following a four-times-a-week schedule when first starting X3:

- Workout 1: Monday and Thursday
- Rest day Wednesday
- Workout 2: Tuesday and Friday
- Rest the entire weekend

Research shows the recovery window for muscular tissue peaks around twenty-four hours after exercise and is only slightly elevated by thirty-six hours.[243] Since the X3 protocol alternates the muscle groups being exercised without any overlap, an every-other-day schedule means each muscle is getting forty-eight hours or longer to recover, which is beyond the thirty-six-hour minimum.

Once you've completed four weeks of the initial X3 protocol, we recommend moving to a six-day-a-week schedule for maximum results. Starting on week five, complete workouts for the first six days of every week and use Sunday as a rest day as follows:

- Workout 1: Monday, Wednesday, and Friday
- Workout 2: Tuesday, Thursday, and Saturday
- Rest on Sunday

ONE SET PER MOVEMENT

With X3, you complete each movement to exhaustion. The deeper level of exhaustion achieved with X3 maximizes the

243 MacDougall, J. D., Gibala, M. J., Tarnopolsky, M. A., MacDonald, J. R., Interisano, S. A., & Yarasheski, K. E. (1995). The time course for elevated muscle protein synthesis following heavy resistance exercise. *Canadian Journal of Applied Physiology*, 20(4), 480-486.

impact of applying the heaviest loads and the benefits of volume training.

Because of the high level of variance provided by X3, typical users can only handle one set per exercise. Therefore, that is our recommendation for the protocol.

A CLOSER LOOK AT MUSCLE GROWTH AND DEVELOPMENT

Before delving into specifics of the X3 set, it is critical to first understand the variables of growth and how they work together in variable-resistance exercise. Here's a closer look at how muscles work, how growth happens, and what maximizes that process.

VOLUME TRAINING

With standard weights, more volume is associated with more growth. But we are not using standard weights, so let's look further at the mechanism of growth.

We know a deeper level of fatigue WITHOUT muscle damage triggers the most growth. The minimum dose-response is critical, as suggested by Carpinelli and Otto (1999).[244] Keeping set numbers low and fatigue high activates this growth phase without subsequent muscle damage, allowing for recovery to be pure growth.

Is there any way, given a more efficient stimulus, we can still have the benefit of more volume? YES, we can. Schoenfeld et al.

---

244 Carpinelli, R., & Otto, R. (1999). Strength training: Single versus multiple sets. *Sports Medicine*, 27(6), 409-416.

(2015) found training each body part three times per week—like the recommended X3 protocol from week five on—with less volume per workout, "suggests a potentially superior hypertrophic benefit to higher weekly resistance training frequencies."[245]

As we've stated before, when trying to gain strength and muscle mass, there is no getting around heavy. Researchers concluded in a 2016 meta-analysis, "a trend was noted for superiority of heavy loading."[246] Heavy loading is only possible in small-volume-type workouts favoring intensity. In addition, more frequent workout session protocols have been shown to provide a volume training effect. That's why we recommend an alternating six-day, push-pull split.

MYOFIBRIL HYPERTROPHY = SPEED AND STRENGTH

An individual muscle is made up of thousands of tube-like muscle fibers (cells) that channel both blood vessels and nerves. Within these fibers are actuators, called myofibrils, which are lined up lengthwise and run the entire length of the cell. Each myofibril is made up of bundles of parallel protein filaments, both thick and thin. This is the structure of the cell, or like the engine as it were. This is the structure that creates the shortening of the muscle in the contraction.

The thick protein filaments, called myosin, have a diameter of approximately fifteen NM (fifteen billionths of a meter). The thin protein filaments, called actin, have a diameter of approx-

---

245 Schoenfeld, B. J., Ratamess, N. A., Peterson, M. D., Contreras, B., & Tiryaki-Sonmez, G. (2015). Influence of resistance training frequency on muscular adaptations in well-trained men. *The Journal of Strength & Conditioning Research*, 29(7), 1821-1829.

246 Schoenfeld, B. J., Wilson, J. M., Lowery, R. P., & Krieger, J. W. (2016). Muscular adaptations in low-versus high-load resistance training: A meta-analysis. *European Journal of Sport Science*, 16(1), 1-10.

imately five NM (five billionths of a meter). The arrangement of this bundle is called a sarcomere. The contraction of the muscle causes the sarcomere to shorten by action of the protein filaments, as shown below:

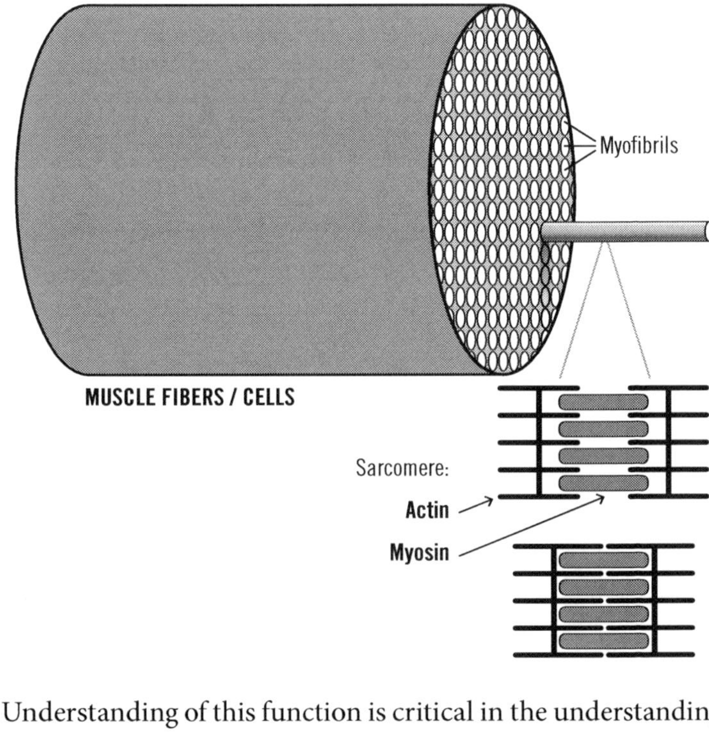

Understanding of this function is critical in the understanding of osteogenic loading, and its comparisons to other exercises. When the structure of the muscle is taken to fatigue and the body begins shutting the myofibrils down towards the end of a weightlifting or X3 set, the muscle can then take free proteins and begin protein synthesis. Having a denser structure enables the instant use of power and can enhance the momentary strength or speed of an athlete.

Vertebrate animals have three different kinds of muscles: skeletal, cardiac, and smooth.

Skeletal muscle, as the name implies, is the muscle attached to the skeletal structure. It is used to convert Adenosine Triphosphate (ATP), the body's standard intracellular energy storage molecule, into physical work. A single skeletal muscle, such as the pectoral muscle, has a tendon attachment at its origin to a large area of bone (in this example, the sternum). At the other end of the muscle, the insertion point is on the humerus. As the pectoral muscle contracts, the insertion point is moved toward the origin and the arm moves closer to the body. This process is controlled by the nervous system.

When at rest, muscle tissue makes demands on all other organs that process nutrients in the adaptation-to-stimulus process. The greater the demands placed on other organs from normal tissue development, the more efficiently they function. During exercise, muscle tissue places demands on the heart and lungs as more oxygenated blood is needed to provide for contractions.

Humans have the greatest control over adaptation of the skeletal muscle, more so than all other organs in the body. You can make positive changes to your health and well-being by improving the function of your skeletal muscles.

SARCOPLASMIC HYPERTROPHY = MUSCULAR SIZE AND ENDURANCE

Sarcoplasmic hypertrophy is sometimes referred to as metabolic stress. Here, the objective is not to create micro-tears but rather to swell the muscles with metabolites, hormones such as testosterone and growth hormone, and other compounds that stimulate more growth and hypertrophy.

How do you trigger this kind of change in your body? By forcing blood to build up in the muscle until there is too much lactic acid to continue. You do this by using higher repetitions, as this allows you to increase "time under tension" (variable tension when using X3)—the length of time your muscle spends contracting during any given workout. While the precise mechanism of action isn't fully understood, this appears to increase the amount of sarcoplasm in the muscle cells. This greater cellular ability to retain fluid and store glycogen enables you to continue lifting for longer and see more growth.

While myofibril hypertrophy leads to increases in size and strength, sarcoplasmic hypertrophy appears to be the fastest way to increase size. For this reason, bodybuilders train with significantly lighter weights but use higher rep ranges, often reaching into the tens of reps with regular weights to focus on sarcoplasmic hypertrophy. By contrast, powerlifters and gymnasts naturally focus on myofibril hypertrophy with lower rep counts and higher forces. This is why a considerably smaller powerlifter will often be able to lift more than a much larger person. But that is not to say that a larger person's muscle isn't as strong or that one type of lifting is better than the other. Furthermore, because of the variance and force curves with variable resistance, we use fifteen to forty repetitions before reaching fatigue while also providing higher-loading forces than are possible with weights, thereby providing aggressive myofibril and sarcoplasmic effects in the same set.

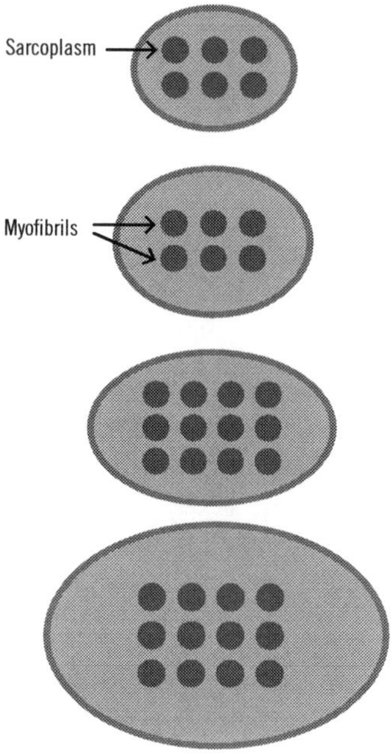

Single muscle cell from an untrained individual, or someone who engages in endurance exercise (non HIIT cardio).

Single muscle cell from an individual who engages in Myofibrils bodybuilding-type training. 3-8 sets 10-12 repetitions, etc. Notice the increase in sarcoplasm.

Single muscle cell from an individual who engages in gymnastics, osteogenic loading therapy, or low rep weight/power lifting. Notice the increase in myofibrils.

Single muscle cell from an individual who engages in the principles in this book. Notice the increase in myofibrils AND sarcoplasm.

LONG-TERM AND SHORT-TERM POTENTIATION

This is the process by which repeated movements involving similar movement patterns can recruit more of the potential cells related to that movement. The more cells/muscle fibers that are involved in the movement, the more stimulation that can occur. A larger percentage of potential muscle fiber engagement can then amplify both myofibril and sarcoplasmic growth, as well as adaptations facilitating increased speed and explosiveness.

PHASES OF AN X3 SET

When working out with X3, there are two distinct phases to each movement.

- **Phase 1:** At the start of a set, users work toward fatigue in the strong range, where high forces promote growth of the myofibrils. Here, you are creating structural fatigue of the muscle but are not yet out of ATP/Glycogen/Creatine phosphate (ATPGCp). This phase is where the most power is built, as the structure of the cell has much more influence on absolute/explosive strength. More tissue is potentiated (called to action), providing the neurological benefit of explosiveness from a different perspective. The hypertrophy in this phase creates musculature with a higher power-to-weight ratio, the most powerful effect of X3. This is comparable to a gymnast's impact absorption-type strength and is driven by the sevenfold greater force output in the impact-ready range, shown in the Hunte, et al. study (2015).[247]

- **Phase 2:** Next, in the same set, the onset of fatigue inhibits the user from reaching the strongest range of motion, and they continue exercising in the lesser ranges (diminishing range). Stores of ATPGCp become depleted and sarcoplasmic fatigue begins. This triggers sarcoplasmic growth and the associated blood flow to recover the muscle. Because a portion of the myofibrils are switched off and a lighter weight is being used during diminished range reps, the muscles are fatigued to a greater degree from both the sarcoplasmic and myofibril perspectives. To compensate for this deeper level of fatigue, the blood flow to recover gets stronger—often referred to as a large pump—which forces a stretching of the fascia. (While this has not been specifically studied with X3, it is the academic understanding of the reaction.) If the principle of constant tension is applied, the hypertrophic effect is greater due to hypoxia. This is because the demand for blood flow, the downregulation of myostatin, and more importantly the replacement and amplification of

247 Hunte, B., Jaquish, J., & Huck, C. (2015). Axial Bone Osteogenic Loading-Type Resistance Therapy Showing BMD and Functional Bone Performance Musculoskeletal Adaptation Over 24 Weeks with Postmenopausal Female Subjects. *Journal of Osteoporosis & Physical Activity*, 3(146), 2.

storing ATPGCp is at its absolute greatest as a result of the hypoxia. The accelerated muscle growth seen with X3 is due to a combination of all of these elements executed to a safer and more powerful degree.

Because both the maximum myofibril and sarcoplasmic effects happen as a result of the same protocol when using X3, there is no need for periodization or alternating light and heavy days.

Periodization has existed in strength sports training for more than fifty years. The basic premise calls for shifting between periods of lighter, higher-volume training (using more sets with lower volume and higher weight) and periods of heavier, lower-volume training. This allows for an alternating focus on a myofibrillar effect (power/density of the muscle cell) and a sarcoplasmic effect (contractile fuel storage of the muscle cell).

Training with regular weights has been shown to have a low myofibril response by Petrella et al. (2008) in the *Journal of American Physiology*. This study analyzed myofibril development in a test group and concluded seventeen out of sixty-six subjects had either no or nominal myofibril response.[248] This suggests that 25 percent of individuals would be wasting their time trying to focus on myofibrillar growth with regular weights.

Of course, this is not the case with variable resistance the way we are applying it.

248 Petrella, J. K., Kim, J. S., Mayhew, D. L., Cross, J. M., & Bamman, M. M. (2008). Potent myofiber hypertrophy during resistance training in humans is associated with satellite cell-mediated myonuclear addition: a cluster analysis. *Journal of Applied Physiology*, *104*(6), 1736-1742.

THE WORKOUT

The X3 protocol employs a push-pull split, a standard weightlifting strategy. One day you do push exercises, the next day you do pull exercises. Research shows the benefits of working synergistic muscles together—meaning the central nervous system responds best to movements that are involved in real-life functional activities.[249]

For example, activating the quadricep muscles almost always means activating the gluteus muscles as well. That's because when moving the lower leg, we tend to also move at the hip joint to maximize the power output and discharge single joint stress. Most of us don't realize this is occurring as it happens subconsciously.

While many muscles work well in single-joint activation like the gastrocnemius and soleus (calves), it is still apparent that more growth happens when muscles are used in a multi-joint activation pattern.

The order in which you do the exercises for that particular day doesn't matter. What's important is grouping the exercises as suggested. Important things to remember for each rep and each set:

1. Follow the instructions in the infographic showcasing the chest press.
2. Slow cadence of repetitions is required. Two seconds up, two seconds down, possibly even three seconds up and down,

249 Gentil, P., Fisher, J. & Steele, J. A (2017). Review of the Acute Effects and Long-Term Adaptations of Single- and Multi-Joint Exercises during Resistance Training. *Sports Med* 47, 843–855.

as shown in research for the maximum muscle thickness growth.[250]

PUSH

Push Day exercises are:

- Chest press
- Tricep press
- Overhead press
- Squats

Chest Press

For chest press, the band is doubled and hooked onto the Olympic bar. The ground plate is not used for this exercise.

Place the doubled band across the back. You can ensure the correct positioning of the band by putting it over your head and one shoulder first so it is crossing your body. Drop the band behind one shoulder, rotate the band slightly, then move your other arm into position. Make sure the band wraps underneath your deltoid.

Proceed in a similar format to any other type of chest-press movement but be sure to keep your elbows flared slightly outward. A forty-five-degree angle is optimal. Focus on bringing the humerus—the upper arm—toward the midline of the body. Keep constant tension so you don't relax at the bottom and you don't lock out of the top. Slow and controlled repetitions are key.

---

250 Nogueira, W., Gentil, P., Mello, S. N. M., Oliveira, R. J., Bezerra, A. J. C., & Bottaro, M. (2009). Effects of power training on muscle thickness of older men. *International journal of Sports Medicine, 30*(03), 200-204.

For example, pictured is John doing chest press using the elite band. He's using the equivalent of 540 pounds at peak force. This is based on his height (six feet tall). NOTE: there is a smartphone application called the X3 Tracker to calculate this for your height.

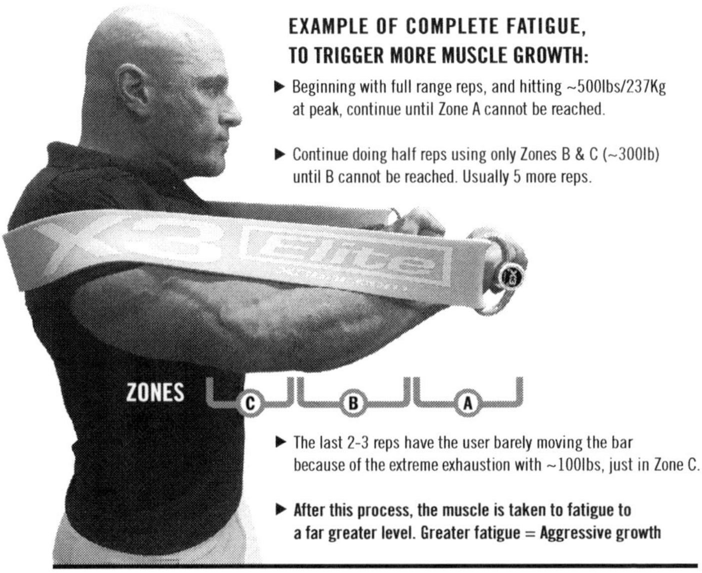

After he has fatigued the stronger range, he starts doing half repetitions. These would equal approximately 300 pounds. His last two or three reps represent extreme exhaustion and happen in Zone C. These are very short repetitions just a few inches from his chest, while still maintaining constant tension.

After this process, the muscle is taken to fatigue to a far greater level. Greater fatigue equals aggressive growth.

Overhead Press

Overhead press works the shoulders and deltoids. For this exercise, the band runs under the ground plate and is hooked to the ends of the Olympic bar. The band is not doubled.

Stand firmly on top of the ground plate. Squat down and rotate your wrists, doing a one-eighty with your hand position. Stand up so the bar is at shoulder height and the band is resting on the outside of the upper arm.

Press the bar slowly overhead, always keeping it in front of you. Never go behind the head, as this causes damage to the shoulder joint. Don't lock out at the top, don't relax at the bottom, and keep constant tension.

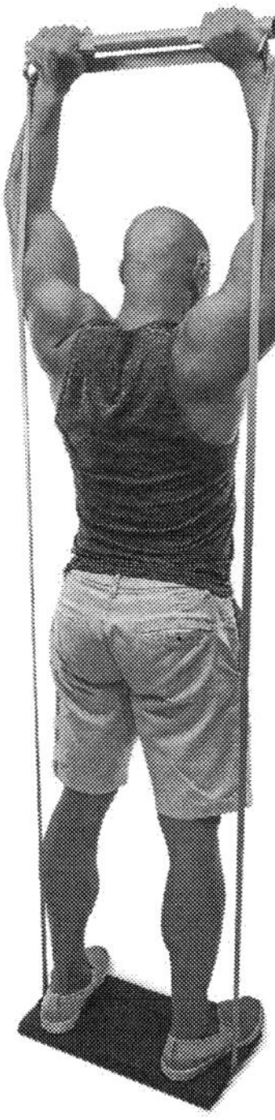

As you become fatigued and are unable to get to the stronger range anymore, begin to work only in the mid-range. As the mid-range diminishes, work in smaller increments until the muscle is fully fatigued.

Some people have a difficult time using the lightest band with the overhead press in the beginning. If that's the case, kneel on the ground plate to complete this exercise. Another option is to purchase an ultra-lightweight band from an outside vendor.

Triceps Press

The band is doubled for this exercise. Run it across your back, a bit higher than where you did for the chest press. The band should cross the center of the deltoid in front.

Start with your arms bent at a ninety-degree angle in front of you and the bar around forehead height. Slowly straighten your arms, hinging only at the elbow. Tuck the elbows in as opposed to flaring them out. The movement should be seen as just hinging at the elbow.

Some people find it easier to complete this exercise hinged forward slightly at the hip. This is also an acceptable form that is often helpful for beginners.

This style of triceps press is often referred to as a "skull crusher" in weightlifting circles. Rest assured, you won't actually hurt your head doing it. Just be sure to use a slow and controlled motion when completing this exercise.

Squats

There are two different ways to perform squats in the X3 protocol. Both types are performed in front squat format because the loading biomechanics are superior there. Back squats create back and shoulder issues. Research confirms this, noting, "The front squat was as effective as the back squat in terms of overall muscle recruitment, with significantly less compressive forces and extensor moments. The results suggest that front squats may be advantageous compared with back squats."[251]

For the first four weeks of doing X3, we recommend doing two-legged squats. For this exercise, the band is singled over and runs under the plate. Grab the bar underneath the band, squat down, and rest the bar on your shoulders. Keep your arms hinged at the elbow and bent up without holding onto the bar.

Drive upward, keeping your elbows pointed forward. Act as if you're sitting in an imaginary chair, keeping your butt back. Do not lock out at the knees and maintain constant tension on the band and muscle. Pay close attention to the knee and toe positioning, making sure the knees never extend over the toes, which would expose the joint to undue stress.

---

251 Gullett, J. C., Tillman, M. D., Gutierrez, G. M., & Chow, J. W. (2009). A biomechanical comparison of back and front squats in healthy trained individuals. *The Journal of Strength & Conditioning Research*, 23(1), 284-292.

After four weeks, you can graduate to split squats, which fire the muscles in one leg at a time. By training in split-squat format, you put all of your body's resources into one glute and one quadriceps. This creates a more powerful muscular response.

With split squats, you stand on one leg with the band running under the mid-foot. Put the other foot back and outside a bit for stability. Because the band only runs under one foot, there is no concern it will twist the ankle inward.

The single squat movement is similar to the two-legged squat. Rest the bar on the shoulders and keep the arms bent, elbows facing forward. Bend at the knee but do not allow the knee to touch the ground. Drive upward in a slow and controlled motion, keeping tension on the band at all times. Keep doing repetitions in a diminishing range until muscle failure, then repeat on the other leg.

PULL DAY

Pull exercises are:

- Deadlift
- Bent row
- Biceps curl
- Calf raise

Deadlift

For this exercise, the band is doubled and lined up under the middle of the ground plate. Stand on top of the ground plate so your mid-foot aligns with the band, bend over with your legs slightly bent at the knee, and hook the band through the bar. We recommend holding the bar with a double overhand Olympic-style grip for this exercise, but you can choose a mixed or underhand grip if that makes the movement more comfortable.

Launch into the movement slowly, focusing on balance. Make sure your center of mass is lined up on top of the band. You're not putting the bar all the way to the ground because at the very bottom, the band is slack and you're in your weakest range of motion. Instead, keep constant tension on the band and your muscle.

Slowly rise up through the motion. Don't lock out your knees at the top. Keep your head and eyes forward, and do not turn your head. Slowly return the band to just below the knees by hinging at the hips. Repeat in a diminishing range of motion until failure.

Bent Row

Once again, the band is doubled and lined up under the middle of the ground plate for this exercise. Stand on top of the ground plate so your mid-foot aligns with the band, bend over with your legs slightly bent at the knee, and hook the band through the bar. We recommend an underhand grip for this exercise.

You remain bent over for the duration of this exercise. Think of the movement as if you're rowing a boat going straight down. Slowly pull the bar into your abdomen, elbows tucked into your sides as opposed to flared out. Do not pull into your chest or back injury can occur. The closer you pull the bar to your hip, the less stress you're placing directly on the back.

The bent row is unusual because it's the only X3 exercise where the range of motion is aligned differently. Normally, out near full extension—the maximum range of motion—is where you're strongest. With the bent row, you're strongest midway through the range of motion. For that reason, it's common to do more partial reps for this exercise. You're not going to be able to pull the bar all the way up to your lower stomach as many times as you'll be able to pull the bar halfway through the range of motion, where force production potential maxes out.

You're going to fatigue very quickly when pulling the bar up into your abdomen. You might have fifteen repetitions that are full range, then twenty-five at mid-range because there is so much more capability in the middle. However, the exercise is just as effective as all the others in the X3 protocol. You're still getting high peak force in your strong range of motion, and you're still protected at the very bottom of the range of motion.

Bicep Curl

For the exercise, the band runs under the ground plate and is hooked to the Olympic bar. Stand with your feet placed firmly in the center of the ground plate.

The movement here is more of a drag curl than a standard bicep curl. A drag curl is when you're almost dragging the bar up the front of your body. This way, you maintain tension through the biceps. Most people rest at the top of a bicep curl without realizing it.

With a drag curl, there's no swing. Keep the bar close to your torso. Do not hold your elbows static at your sides but move them backwards as the bar comes up. Complete as many full and partial repetitions as you can until exhaustion.

Calf Raises

For this exercise, the band is doubled under the ground plate and hooked onto the Olympic bar. Step onto the ground plate with your heels hanging off the back. The toe and ball of the foot should be in line with the band.

Get into a similar position as the top of a deadlift. From this standing position, contract your calves. Keep the feet parallel to one another as you raise and lower your heels. Do not allow your heels to touch the ground, ensuring constant force on the muscle throughout the range of motion.

Like the deadlift, this exercise requires balance, as forces are high and you're on your toes. Go slow and be careful. Continue from full repetitions to partial until you've reached absolute fatigue.

CUSTOMIZATION

The X3 protocol is fast, easy to follow, and highly effective. There are four exercises each day, alternating every day, completed in approximately ten minutes. There's a tendency for people to want to overcomplicate the workout because they think it is too simple. Most often, this leads to worse results, not better, so don't overcomplicate things.

However, for a minority of users with specific needs, usually previous injury, there is the option to add or subtract certain movements.

Additional Push Movement: The Crossover

For added thickness in pectorals, the crossover can be completed after the chest press. This is similar to doing a cable crossover with a lighter band. This optional movement is more of a bodybuilding than a functional exercise.

To complete this exercise, wrap the band around your back and hold the ends in your hands. The band should cross the center of your deltoid.

Slowly extend the arms in front of and across your body, alternating which hand crosses over the top of the other during each repetition to ensure symmetry. Stop just before you lock the elbows out with your arms overlapping in front of you in the shape of an X.

Stay strong and controlled throughout the movement. Do as many full repetitions as possible, then work in diminishing range until you've reached full muscular fatigue.

The most pectoral activation comes as the humerus crosses the midline of the body. When the crossover is done immediately following the chest press, there is added fatigue and blood flow sent directly to the pectoral muscle.

OMITTING SPECIFIC EXERCISES

The additional customizations reflect exercises you may want to leave out of your workout rather than any other additions. For example, Ben Greenfield of the podcast Ben Greenfield Fitness likes to focus only on what he calls "functional exercises." The exact definition of this is subject to different perspectives.

Ben would likely argue that a bent row is a functional exercise—one that emulates a natural body movement in a non-fitness context—since that's how you'd naturally pick up a heavy item while a bicep curl is not. On the other hand, John thinks that for those less experienced in fitness, it can be misleading to suggest a bicep curl is non-functional, since it is meant to elicit a contraction of the bicep and it could be argued that when a muscle shortens, that's its function.

When Ben was interviewing John, he asked why we included exercises that are not considering functional like the bicep curl in the X3 protocol. John told him flat out, "Vanity." Is doing specific calf work going to make you better at your job? Probably not, but you will look better in shorts.

Some other examples of groups that might want to omit certain exercises from the X3 protocol include CrossFitters and marathoners. CrossFit competitors might not want to do single-joint movements like tricep presses, bicep curls, and calf raises since their sport does not emphasize these. Ultra-marathoners might skip bicep curls, since having strong arms does not add to the experience of endurance running.

This all said, we recommend that a vast majority of people follow the standard X3 protocol for optimal results. However, if your goals don't require certain movements and you skip those exercises, you will still get benefits from the remaining ones. No particular movement is obligatory, and choosing only those that apply to your endeavors won't prevent you from getting results from X3.

X3 AND OTHER ATHLETIC ENDEAVORS

We recommend if you are doing another athletic event on the same day as X3, you should do X3 first. While the X3 workout is very short, achieving complete fatigue takes energy and willpower you may not possess after another physical challenge.

The goal is to get as much as possible out of your one X3 set. When you're tired, you may not have the ability to push through and make the most of your session.

Although performing an X3 workout is not going to hurt your endurance, we recommend skipping your session if you are going to be competing that day. Save your energy and focus for your other athletic endeavor. Hit X3 hard again the next day.

For scientific updates in physiology, sports science, nutrition, invitations to lectures, and general optimization of human performance, follow Dr. Jaquish on social media:

Facebook: Dr. John Jaquish
Instagram: @drjaquish

ACKNOWLEDGMENTS

First of all, we'd like to thank Trish Cook, who carefully worked with us on the (seemingly) endless revisions and additions to our manuscript.

We'd also like to thank Libby Allen, our publishing manager, who made sure the whole book actually came together, as well as Aspen Drake and Julia Krigbaum, who helped proofread and edit our drafts.

Thanks to Tucker Max, who carved out some of his time to talk with us when we still weren't sure if we were going to write this book and provided the encouragement required for us to get started.

Thanks also to Dr. Shawn Baker for sharing the research, anecdotes, and logic behind his paradigm-shifting perspective on nutrition, which certainly influenced the discussion in this book.

It was Kyle Zagrodzky's efforts to globally deploy our Spectrum osteogenic loading device that launched us into this journey, and for that, he has our gratitude. We are grateful to Tony Robbins as well, who has partnered with Kyle on that worthy endeavor.

Alan Guinn contributed substantially to Dr. Jaquish's education and helped him learn to look past the orthodoxy in some scientific circles and evaluate research in an objective manner. Thank you, Alan, for providing me with that background; it was a necessary foundation for the research that went into this book.

And we owe a special 'Thank You' to Jason Young, Todd Stratton, John Ferro, and Maykell Lorenzo for telling their stories about their success with our training method and allowing us to include them in this book. Your hard work and bold examples go a long way towards demonstrating the reality behind the theories put forth in this book, and we appreciate the help.

For this same reason, we'd like to thank all of the long-term X3 users who have invested large amounts of time sharing their experience and progress with us and with others on social media, including Brandon Witters, David Fish, Jeff Grobe, Karen ODonnell, Bobby Foerster, George Hayworth, Dr. Raghav Tadepalli, and everyone who has contributed to our online communities. We appreciate all of the positive feedback, and beyond that, seeing your real-world success with our principles is deeply rewarding and reaffirms our belief that the arguments in this book can be of great value to others and are worth sharing with the world.

ABOUT THE AUTHORS

JOHN JAQUISH, PHD, is the inventor of the most effective bone-density building medical device, as confirmed through research conducted by NASA Human Performance Research Center at the University of Texas Medical School. John is now partnered with Tony Robbins for rapid clinical deployment of OsteoStrong, which has reversed osteoporosis in thousands and created more powerful, fracture-resistant users. In the process of his medical research, Dr. Jaquish quantified the variance in power capacities from weak to strong ranges in weightlifting, which led to his second invention, X3. Research indicates X3 builds muscle much faster than conventional lifting in far less training time and at the lowest risk of joint injury. Dr. Jaquish has been called "the Tony Stark of the Fitness Industry" by the *Chicago Tribune*. He has been featured on many of the top health podcasts and speaks at scientific conferences all over the world. Dr. Jaquish is an editor of multiple medical journals, a nominee of the National Medal of Science, and a research professor at Rushmore University, his alma mater.

HENRY ALKIRE is a biomedical engineer and lifelong tinkerer who likes cars and coffee. He has been working with John

Jaquish since 2012 to perform just about every kind of engineering, draft patents, author scientific research, and create and launch advertising campaigns. He lives in the foothills of Northern California, where he can be found experimenting with making new devices because "no one else makes it and he wants one."

Printed in Great Britain
by Amazon

0c1ad57b-3aec-433e-b84d-93e0442d44c2R01